Peter Fairbrother is a lecturer in sociology at the University of Warwick. He has been a tutor in trade union education for many years.

Peter Fairbrother

All Those in Favour
The Politics of Union Democracy

London and Sydney

First published in 1984 by
Pluto Press Limited
The Works, 105a Torriano Avenue
London NW5 2RX
and Pluto Press Australia Limited
PO Box 199, Leichhardt
New South Wales 2040, Australia

Copyright © Peter Fairbrother, 1984

Photoset and printed in Great Britain by
Photobooks (Bristol) Ltd.
Bound by W. H. Ware, Tweed Road, Clevedon

British Library Cataloguing in Publication Data

Fairbrother, Peter
 All those in favour.
 1. Trade-unions——Great Britain
 2. Trade-unions——Great Britain——Voting
 I. Title
 331.87   HD6664

ISBN 0-86104-763-X

Contents

Preface / vii

Acknowledgements / viii

Abbreviations / ix

1. Crisis / 1

2. Legislating for 'Reform' / 6

3. Definitions of Union Democracy / 23

4. Debates about Union Democracy / 31

5. Many Ways to Ballot the Membership / 42

6. Representing Members / 50

7. Economics and Politics: The Fateful Separation / 63

8. What Is Wrong with Unions? / 70

9. The Basis of Union Democracy / 83

10. Unions in the Workplace / 88

11. National Union Organization / 96

12. Union Democracy and Socialism / 105

   A Guide to Reading / 110

Preface

This book is about the politics of union democracy. The issues discussed are crucial for trade unionism and socialism. There are no quick and immediate answers to many of the problems identified in the book. But as a first step toward union democracy these issues must be debated and discussed by trade unionists. This is the beginning of union democracy.

At the time of writing, the Tories have issued a major challenge to unions. Currently the Trade Union Bill 1983 is going through the House of Commons. It is now in the committee stage, having completed its Second Reading. Present indications are that the Bill will reach the statute books, virtually intact, some time before October 1984. Some tactical amendments may be made so as to create the impression of a government prepared to listen to unions, although any concession is likely to be minimal. What is clear is that the threat to unions will not be minimized.

The TUC has responded to the Bill by defending union practice and reluctantly acquiescing to Tory demands. As part of this response the TUC published a *TUC Strategy* (January 1984), prepared under the guidance of Lionel Murray, for consideration by the TUC General Council. Whilst the document says little that is new, its significance lies in the assertion of the view that the TUC must be willing to deal with all governments, and that unions must be willing to look again at their organization and practices. The response by unions to this initiative remains to be seen.

Union democracy is a crucial issue for the working class. After all, unions are the only mass-based organisations in Britain today. They are potentially the principal means whereby workers can defend and extend their interests. More than this, union democracy is a prerequisite of socialism. This is the case I argue in this book.

Acknowledgements

This book is the product of many debates and discussions about union democracy. For me, these first began as a student in Australia. I still remain in the debt of Bill Howard and Di Yerbury who showed me so long ago that there was no easy path to union democracy.

From 1979 to 1982 I was fortunate to be a member of a research team which looked at the structure and organization of the Society of Civil and Public Servants. Peter Drake, Bob Fryer, Jeanette Murphy and Geoff Stratford provided an exciting, demanding and sometimes heated milieu in which to explore ideas about union democracy. During this time I learnt a lot from all the members of the union who were willing to engage in debate and discussion about the union and who made me think, and think again. I would also like to thank Mel Doyle of the Workers' Educational Association who, following this research, encouraged me to write a booklet on union ballots. This provided me with an opportunity to develop further the arguments for union democracy and lay the foundation for this book.

My first immediate debt is to John Harrison who convinced me that I had the time to write. Thanks are also due to Michelle Murch who loaded the first draft on to computer, quickly and efficiently, thereby making the book a possibility. Subsequently, the following gave generously of their time to comment on the arguments presented in the book: Simon Clarke, Tony Elger, John Fisher, and Geoff Stratford. I would especially like to thank Michael Terry who set aside much time to read and re-read the manuscript and to discuss the arguments with me. I want also to thank Richard Kuper for his patient, sensitive and supportive advice during the writing of the book.

In keeping with a book about union democracy, I was forced, through debate and discussion, to defend, alter and elaborate my views on the subject. To this extent, all the above are responsible for the views presented in the book.

Abbreviations

ACTSS	Association of Clerical, Technical and Supervisory Staff
ACTT	Association of Cinematograph, Television and Allied Technicians
APEX	Association of Professional, Executive, Clerical and Computer Staff
ASLEF	Associated Society of Locomotive Engineers and Firemen
ASTMS	Association of Scientific, Technical and Managerial Staffs
AUEW	Amalgamated Union of Engineering Workers
AUEW (ES)	Amalgamated Union of Engineering Workers: Engineering Section
AUT	Association of University Teachers
BALPA	British Airline Pilots' Association
BIFU	Banking, Insurance and Finance Union
BL	British Leyland
COHSE	Confederation of Health Service Employees
CPSA	Civil and Public Services' Association
DE	Department of Employment
EETPU	Electrical, Electronic, Telecommunication and Plumbing Union
GMBATU	General Municipal, Boilermakers' and Allied Trades' Union
GMWU	General and Municipal Workers' Union
IRSF	Inland Revenue Staff Federation
ISTC	Iron and Steel Trades Confederation
LRD	Labour Research Department
NALGO	National and Local Government Officers' Association
NATFHE	National Association of Teachers in Further and Higher Education
NGA	National Graphical Association
NUJ	National Union of Journalists
NUM	National Union of Mineworkers

NUPE	National Union of Public Employees
NUR	National Union of Railwaymen
NUS	National Union of Seamen
NUT	National Union of Teachers
POEU	Post Office Engineering Union
SCPS	Society of Civil and Public Servants
SDP	Social Democratic Party
SOGAT 82	Society of Graphical and Allied Trades
TASS	Amalgamated Union of Engineering Workers: Technical Administrative and Supervisory Section
TGWU	Transport and General Workers' Union
TSSA	Transport Salaried Staffs' Association
TUC	Trades Union Congress
TWU	Tobacco Workers' Union
UCATT	Union of Construction, Allied Trades and Technicians
UCW	Union of Communication Workers
USDAW	Union of Shop, Distributive and Allied Workers

1. Crisis

Trade unions are in crisis: Tory legislation threatens to destabilize and demobilize unions and there has been little more than a muted response from most union leaders. Initially the response from the Trade Union Congress (TUC) and the Labour Party was one of incredulity, followed by complaints about fairness, and now reluctant acquiescence. That any government should feel sufficiently confident to act in this way is testimony to the fact that something is very wrong with organized labour. That these assaults are 'populist' is in itself paradoxical: the object is to destabilize the only organizations in British society with a mass base and with the potential ability to challenge the state.

The Tory threat

The argument in this book is presented in response to the current Tory attack on trade unions. The Tory government aims to shape and control unions so that they are no longer able to provide a potential focus for mass organization and action. They seek to achieve this through legislation as well as by creating an economic environment and a propaganda campaign to weaken and demobilize unions. In this regard, the Tories have been relatively successful.

The current legislation is but the latest version of a whole string of proposals aimed at controlling unions. As far back as 1958 a group of Conservative lawyers penned *A Giant's Strength* in which they bemoaned the apparent power of trade unions. They asserted that unions were too powerful, that they were a fourth estate, and a potential threat to the orderly working of society. So they called for the curtailment and control of unions. Although it was not until the 1970s that this 'concern' was translated into legislation, the Tories have continued to cling to the belief that unions are too powerful.

During the 1970s the Tories discovered a 'lack' of democracy in unions. More correctly, they found an absence of Tory democracy. The call went out: unions do not represent members; ordinary decent workers do not have a say in their unions; union bosses run and control unions; the left are in control; moderates are on the run; and so on. But behind the rhetoric Tories still had one concern: how to control unions.

What is different today is that the Tories have passed two anti-union Acts and are now legislating a third. If the union campaigns continue as at present, then this legislation is likely to remain on the statute books for at least another three or four years. Should this happen, unions will be further weakened as effective working-class organizations able to articulate and defend working-class interests and concerns. This is the threat they face.

An indolent response

Union leaders have sought refuge behind arguments about the viciousness of this government, the sustained attacks from the media, or the debilitation by mass unemployment of effective trade unionism. They have not faced up to the fact that the Tory offensive has widespread popular appeal. The weakness of the official union responses to these threats requires explanation; such is the aim of this book. In it I seek to explain what has been 'forgotten' within the movement about the principles and practice of trade unions. I examine why trade unionism has fallen into disrepute even among union members. In doing this I consider why unions have been caught unawares and are unable to respond effectively to these threats.

Union responses to the current challenge have been very much shaped by the past. Unions have looked back to the campaigns against the Tory Industrial Relations Act 1971 as confirmation of the potential they have to defeat legislation. At the time the Tory claim that managers have the right to manage was countered by arguments that this would not contribute to good industrial relations. Such a holding position is not argued by unions today. Moreover, mass campaigning against the legislation has been rejected by the TUC.

Unions have relied on a bald claim that they are 'naturally' democratic to counter claims to the contrary. In this, union leaders have pointed to the varied balloting procedures evident in unions and the diverse forms of accountability and representation as testimony to their democratic faith and practice. But this is a limited defence, and even more so when it is presented simply as a defence of the right of unions to conduct their affairs as they see fit.

Unions have also looked back to the golden days of the 'social contract' period (1974–79) as a time of 'reasonable' government. This was a time when union leaders and the government worked in harmony and close co-operation, at least until 1978. But the reliance of trade unions on benevolent Labour governments to maintain their interests was already becoming thin by the end of the 1970s. This is now a major cause of their weakness when they have to turn to their membership for support.

Whilst Labour governments have not attempted to coerce unions as the Tories have done, they have attempted to mould them and encourage 'responsible' union leadership. That is, Labour governments have attempted to encourage union leaders prepared to argue and support Labour policies and programmes. This is justified by the belief that the different interests of labour and capital can be reconciled and that a fairer and more equitable society can be achieved through parliamentary initiative and decree. But even when a Labour government is elected, it soon finds itself faced by the power of capital. It is then forced to subordinate its social aims to the attempt to achieve the efficient management of a capitalist society. And Labour governments attempt to achieve this only too vigorously.

The case for union democracy

So what are unions to do? It is my view that they can no longer rely on past practice or hope for a fairer future. Instead, they must face up to the threat posed by the Tories and start rebuilding in accordance with the principles of union democracy. Only in this way will they be able to realize their promise as mass organizations able to challenge state policy and practice as well as employers. But more than this, it is by developing democratic unions that the foundation is laid for socialism. Just as union democracy is characterized by participation, so too is socialism.

I shall argue that there are ways of organizing which will allow or enable democratic unionism to develop and flourish. It is not a blueprint: my concern is to clarify and specify the principles that should underpin all union organization and activity. Obviously, the circumstances and conditions of organization differ from one union to another, which means that it may be possible to realize some principles of union democracy while still striving for others. It will become clear that left-wing advocates of union democracy often face difficult choices about the principles they should support at any one time. Where appropriate I have indicated the choices I would make. I have written the book in the belief that union democracy is about debate and discussion, agreement and disagreement, and collective decision and discipline. So too, the choices we confront and the decisions we make in our fight for union democracy are part of what that democracy is all about.

I reject the prevalent view being canvassed that there are many paths to democracy; too often this has become an excuse for not looking beyond particular organizational forms and structures to the principles which underpin them. We must develop the argument that union democracy is distinctive: as a form of participatory structures and organization and as a condition for the achievement of socialism. It is in these terms that unions can be important agents in the struggle between labour and capital and also in taking the first tentative steps toward achieving a socialist society.

This, then, is a book about 'forgotten' union principles. It is about union democracy, its form and content; it is about the importance of union democracy for trade union members and the working class. I argue that today the working class can defend itself only through union organization and action, organized and operating in a democratic way. More than this, in advanced capitalist societies where the prospects for socialism look so bleak, it is my contention that unions are potentially one of the very few vehicles for advancing socialist ideas and practice. So this is also a book about the practice of socialist struggle in capitalist societies.

Plan of the book

I begin by looking, in Chapter 2, at the threats that state policies have posed to trade unions. I detail the current Tory legislative proposals, and place them in their historical context. This is then complemented by a consideration of the meanderings of the Labour Party which show how the policy of union autonomy has become an attractive option. Finally, I briefly detail the Social Democratic–Liberal Party Alliance stance on union 'reform'.

Against this background Chapter 3 looks at the different claims made for union democracy by politicians and union leaders. First of all, however, I specify union democracy as I understand it. This is the benchmark against which I assess and evaluate trade union policies and practice. I then consider the way in which the issue of union democracy has been taken up by both politicians and union leaders and has become a question of union autonomy rather than union democracy. Unfortunately, this has meant that the principles of union democracy have not been developed and elaborated.

In Chapter 4 I consider the major issues raised in debates about union democracy, in particular the prominence given to voting and the circumstances for membership participation and involvement. Whilst a number of important questions have been raised in these debates, this has often been on the basis of a cursory consideration of union practice.

In the following two Chapters, 5 and 6, I look at current union practice, focusing on ballots and forms of representation. Clearly there are a variety of practices and procedures followed by unions. Still, some common features are evident. Workplace stewards are an integral part of most union structures, which suggests that there is a ready base upon which to build and develop these structures. However, there is also evidence to show that at a local and a national level elected and appointed officials are not always accountable to and under the control of the membership.

Union concerns are principally with 'economic' matters. As I shall detail in Chapter 6, many unions officially adopt a view that 'politics' is best left to the politicians, preferably Labour Party members. To this extent the fateful distinction drawn by many union members between 'economics' (the province of unions) and 'politics' (the province of the Labour Party) is reaffirmed. Nonetheless, there are some signs that a few unions, through their campaigns and actions, have begun to recognize the inextricable link between 'politics' and 'economics', albeit in a tentative way.

In Chapter 8 I draw the threads of the argument together by focusing on the very real problems with unions today. I argue that too often they are divided and concerned with limited objectives. This is most clearly brought out in relation to gender divisions, in that women are more or less systematically excluded from major union activities and offices. Linked to this, unions tend to be dominated by national officials and are reformist in their approach to change and progress.

Any consideration of the principles of union democracy must begin with a consideration of the circumstances and conditions in which unions organize. In Chapter 9 I examine the employment relations to which unions must necessarily relate. I then analyse the class basis of trade unionism, drawing attention to the way in which class relations underpin the movement.

In Chapters 10 and 11 I set down the principles of union democracy. I argue that unions must be organized in the workplace around workplace stewards, accountable to and controlled by union members. Only under these circumstances is it possible for unions to rebuild on the basis of membership involvement and participation. Following on from this I argue that these principles of organization, accountability and control should guide union structure and practice at all other levels. Significantly, this would require a reassessment of current union organization and practice, especially the relation between general secretaries and executive committees.

Finally, in Chapter 12, I consider the link between union democracy and socialism. I argue that the fight for union democracy is also a fight for socialism. More than this, I claim that union democracy signifies the possibility and hope of socialism.

2. Legislating for 'Reform'

The stated aim of postwar party policies about trade unions has been one of 'reform'. In this context 'reform' has been presented as making union leaderships more responsive to members through alternative decision-making processes. There are both weak and strong versions of this reform philosophy. The strong version sees trade unions needing 'reform' but unwilling to 'reform' themselves; so it becomes the responsibility of governments to legislate change. Most recently both the Conservative Party and the Social Democratic Party (SDP) have advocated this version. The weaker version is that 'reform' is desirable but legal compulsion is not, so if unions request state assistance then governments should be willing to consider such requests and introduce appropriate legislation. This is the current Labour Party position.

Over the last 35 years there have been important shifts in the issues addressed by political parties. During the 1950s and 1960s attention was directed more toward strike ballots and less toward elections. More recently, attention has concentrated on elections, and in particular the importance of postal ballots for the election of national union representatives. To an important extent, this has been associated with a reassessment of the value of strike ballots, namely that while desirable they may not achieve the ends desired by policy-makers.

With regard to ballot procedures, there has been frequent confusion about the type of ballot considered. Two features of ballots have been examined: their secrecy and their form. Often in the course of advocating particular ballot procedures there has been a shift in the argument from secret ballots in general to postal ballots in particular. Recently, attention has been focused almost exclusively on postal ballots, even when reference has been made to secret ballots. In addition, there has been vagueness about the definition of postal ballots.

Conservative Party: What is new?

Current policies
Trade unionism has always been regarded as a problem by the Conservative Party. In the past this has led to the party advocating legal

restrictions on trade union activity. More recently, the party has been concerned to restructure trade unions, expressed as a call for 'democracy' in trade unions. The preferred means is the secret postal ballot.

The new emphasis in Tory policy represents a break with the past. Prior to the Second World War, Conservative policy was overtly anti-union. The object was to demobilize and repress unions, thereby providing the conditions for restructuring economic and social relations. After the Second World War there was tacit acceptance that unions should be a partner (albeit subordinate) in reconstruction. The postwar policy was celebrated in the ideology of 'one-nation' articulated by Conservative and Labour governments, although with important differences in emphasis. However, as the social contradictions of production in the 1960s and 1970s deepened, this policy was rejected. An attempt is now being made to undermine the collective strength of trade unions through a reassertion of individualism.

The post-1979 Conservative government has issued a number of statements about trade unions, the most comprehensive being the 1982 Green Paper, *Democracy in Trade Unions*, which set the tone for the 1983 White Paper, *Proposals for Legislation in Trade Unions*, and the *Trade Union Bill*, 1983. What sets it apart from earlier postwar sentiments is the rejection of the language of co-operation and 'responsible' union behaviour. Increasingly the Conservative Party has stressed the need for internal union 'reform' and individual membership control over union activities.

The Green Paper encapsulates the emphasis in Tory thinking from the mid 1970s onwards. Two issues are examined: the internal arrangements of trade unions and their political relationships, particularly with the Labour Party.

With regard to the internal arrangements of trade unions, two issues are considered: trade union elections and ballots before strikes. In the case of elections, change is advocated on the grounds that union leaders are out of touch with their members. The problem is that without legislation unions would not 'reform' themselves; so the government would consider legislation to compel change. It is argued that the most appropriate way to make union leaders more representative of members and directly responsible to them is through secret postal ballots. In contrast with previous statements on general secretaries, the case for the election of these officers is not developed. Instead, it is suggested that general secretaries and other full-time officers should be elected or appointed, depending on the needs and requirements of the union. It is also suggested that there may be a case for periodic election where general secretaries have been elected in the first instance or where they have a vote on the governing body.

Another claim is that there is a strong case for ballots before strikes. The underlying assumption is that current procedures for consultation about strike action in trade unions are 'often totally inadequate'. Three issues are considered:

whether such ballots should be made compulsory by law;
how compulsion might be achieved;
the effects of such legislation in practice.

On the basis of an examination of these three issues, three proposals are examined:

strike ballots imposed by the state in specific circumstances;
strike ballots which are 'triggered' by a specified proportion of members;
strike ballots which are 'triggered' by the employer.

On this question there is a strong suggestion that the government favours strike ballots which will be 'triggered' by either trade union members or employers. Of the two, there seemed to be a preference for employer ballots. The arguments are based on an assumption that trade union members have minimal influence within their unions. On this basis it is claimed that unions often pursue policies which reflect neither the views nor the interests of members.

Unions and politics

On the second major issue, the argument is developed that the concerns of unions should be restricted to industrial issues alone, the current arrangement for members to contract out of the political levy being replaced by a provision to contract in. It also proposes that the rules for political funds be extended to include non-party activities, and to change the rules on check-off in order to make the collecting of dues for the political levy more difficult. While this section of the paper is directed toward the financial basis of the Labour Party, it is also aimed at making it more difficult for unions to pursue their political concerns and campaigning activities. This complements the definition of lawful trade disputes under the Employment Act 1982 which outlawed 'political strikes'.

Legislative proposals

Following the 1983 election, the re-elected Conservative government moved quickly to introduce legislation broadly along the lines canvassed in the Green Paper. On 12 July 1983, a White Paper, *Proposals for Legislation on Democracy in Trade Unions*, was published; it was followed by the Trade Union Bill on 26 October 1983. The key recommendations are outlined below.

First, union executives and voting general secretaries should be elected through a secret national ballot, possibly a postal ballot. Although the venue for these ballots is not specified, the Bill states that every member should have a 'fair and convenient opportunity to vote' at no direct cost to the member. Significantly, the onus of enforcement is placed on members, namely by applying to courts for enforcement of these statutory proposals. All members of such executives should be elected or re-elected at least once every five years.

Second, unions henceforth will be required to ballot all members being called out on strike or more accurately, on any industrial action which results in a breach of contract. Such a ballot must include all members 'whom it is reasonable to believe' will be involved in this action, and no one else. If unions do not do this, or the ballot is held more than four weeks before action, then the civil law immunity will be removed and the union could be sued for an injury, with claims being made on union funds. As with elections, such ballots should be secret and there should be an equal and unrestricted right to vote.

Third, the Bill introduces a number of regulations aimed at the political activities of unions. Ballots on the continuation of political funds are required once every ten years and the definition of 'political' activity is broadened so as to make a wider variety of activities subject to these regulations.

These proposals are aimed at destabilizing and devaluing unions. This is to be achieved first through election procedures for members of principal union executive committees. The Tory hope is that unions will come to be led by cautious leaders who will abide by the law; the Tories are opposed to the collective consideration of candidates for the senior office. In this way, the Tories hope that a generation of leaders will emerge who will be more in accord with the less involved and committed member than with the union activist. Second, these proposals are to place a series of obstacles in the way of strikes and other industrial action. These obstacles include regulation and the creation of uncertainty in the minds of members about strike action. A further consequence of these proposals would be to focus the attention of the union on the strike ballot rather than the organization of the strike itself. Finally, through limitations on the 'political' activity of unions, the Tories aim to restrict the way in which unions pursue the interests of their members. Additionally, these regulations aim to limit unions' contributions to and support of the Labour Party. Taken together, this is a comprehensive challenge to union organization and activity.

Strike ballots

One way of following through these recent changes in emphasis is to focus on the way in which attention has been directed toward ballot procedures and a search for 'acceptable' strike ballots. To do this, it is necessary to go back to the 1958 Conservative Party lawyers' pamphlet, *A Giant's Strength*, which summarized the practical and ideological concerns of Conservative Party thinking on trade unionism at the time.

A Giant's Strength claimed that trade unions were powerful institutions which should be restrained. Particular concern was expressed about strikes, specifically secondary, sympathetic or political strikes. Legislation to compel ballots before strikes was discussed but rejected, although ballots 'triggered' by members opposed to the continuation of a strike were endorsed. Two problems were noted. First, there was a recognition that such ballots might encourage members to support strike calls and might make negotiators more intransigent. Second, strike ballots might make unofficial strikes more likely as a means of bypassing statutory ballots. Practically, it would be difficult to organize as well as being open to abuse, particularly through the wording of questions put to members. Nevertheless, it was suggested that ballots should occur if requested by a proportion of members who wished to call off a strike.

The experience of the Labour government in dealing with trade unions during the 1960s gave rise to a view within the Conservative Party that unions must be controlled more directly. With the development of relatively confident workplace trade unionism in some industries, particularly engineering, it appeared to some that unions were out of control. The strategy advocated by the Tories was twofold: to put pressure on national union leaderships to control the activity of rank-and-file members, and to restrict and control the activity of workplace union members. It was an attempt to demobilize unions through two seemingly contradictory policies: first, an attempt to incorporate or make union leaders responsible for the activities of their members, and, second, to undermine collective organization by introducing individual responsibility and decision-making into union affairs.

This view was at the heart of the 1969 policy, *Fair Deal At Work*. Its proposals included:

> the use of secret postal ballots in elections;
> the use of secret ballots to decide whether to accept the employer's last offer when a dispute endangers the 'national interest';
> the use of ballots to determine if a majority of workers at a place of work are in favour of union recognition.

These proposals were part of a 'new approach to industrial relations' which would contribute to improved and increased industrial efficiency. To achieve this goal 'responsible' trade unionism and constitutional union authority had to be encouraged and strengthened.

The greater use of ballots by trade unions was also provided for in the Industrial Relations Act 1971, although on a relatively limited scale, in the following areas: national emergencies; union recognition; closed shops.

This 1971 Act did not require the use of secret postal ballots; nor did it require that the principle of elections be extended to include appointed full-time officers. It did not even require that votes be taken by secret ballot, although it was stipulated that if ballots were held they should be kept secret. These were important omissions and they signified the dilemma faced by the Conservative Party: trade unions were a power to be reckoned with and they were a power that should be curtailed.

The 1972 railways dispute
The provisions relating to strike ballots were used once, during the railways dispute in 1972. On this occasion, the then Conservative government decided to intervene in a pay dispute between the railway unions and British Railways Board. Briefly, following the breakdown of pay negotiations on 17 April 1972, the unions commenced a work-to-rule and overtime ban. The initial response by the government was to make a successful application to the National Industrial Relations Court for a compulsory 'cooling-off' period, which ran from 25 April to 8 May 1972. When this failed to achieve a resolution of the dispute, the government made a further application to the court, this time for a compulsory ballot of railway workers about the action. The grounds for the application were that further action by the unions would 'be gravely injurious to the national economy'. Following an appeal which upheld the court decision to order a ballot, a postal ballot of railway workers was conducted by the Commission on Industrial Relations. The vote was more than five to one in favour of further action. Shortly after, before any further industrial action, the dispute was settled, with a slightly increased pay offer.

The Commission chose to conduct the ballot as a postal one, although there was no legal requirement to do so. The result was a lesson for the Conservative Party. It appeared to confirm the views expressed in *A Giant's Strength* that ballots about industrial action may serve to strengthen a militant stance rather than undermine it. More generally, this dispute was seen to demonstrate the inadequacies of legislative compulsion. The lesson that the Conservative Party took from this episode was that the state should not be directly involved in the enforcement of laws on trade union activity. With the successful passage of the Trade Union Bill 1983, enforcement will be the responsibility of members and employers, not the state.

Postal ballots for elections

Following electoral defeat for the Conservatives in 1974, and its repercussions within the party, a new emphasis emerged in policy toward organized labour. Election procedures in TUC unions were deemed unsatisfactory and in need of improvement by legislation. The 1974 Conservative Party manifesto had pledged to do this if the party were returned to office. This commitment was subsequently affirmed in 1975 by the then Shadow Minister for Employment, James Prior. It was reaffirmed in the 1976 party manifesto, *The Right Approach*. Two facets were identified: low participation in union meetings and the unrepresentativeness of many trade union leaders. This, it was claimed, reflected a lack of democracy in unions, or, at best, imperfect democratic procedures. This linking of ballots and democracy became increasingly central to the debate about secret postal ballots.

After re-election to office in 1979, the Conservative Party proceeded to translate its pledges into law. The Employment Act 1980 made provision for a legal right to workplace ballots. Subsequently the Secretary of State introduced a regulation providing for funds for secret postal ballots in trade union elections and for the calling and ending of industrial action. In 1981 the government Green Paper, *Trade Union Immunities*, anticipated legislation to encourage the greater use of secret ballots before industrial action. In addition, it was asserted that it was desirable that the use of postal ballots be extended to include membership consultation and the election of trade union leaders. On 1 September 1982 the current provisions were extended to allow unions to claim back the cost of secret postal ballots held to decide pay offers.

Membership ballots

The Conservative government has also given notice to the trade union movement of a major extension of ballots on union membership agreements. Membership ballots are already a feature of union and employment law. They have been required for the consideration of union mergers and the establishment of political funds. Apart from provisions in the Industrial Relations Act 1971, it has been usual to leave unions to decide their own ballot procedures in the light of their specific concerns and circumstances. However, in the Employment Act 1980 and 1982 provision was made for ballots on the continuation of closed shop agreements. Briefly, this meant it would be unfair for an employer to dismiss a worker for non-union membership by way of enforcing a closed shop agreement if no ballot had been held to ratify the agreement. For this provision to be made effective the Secretary of State has only to issue an order on the subject (expected to be effective from 1 November 1984). This opens up the prospect of widespread ballots on closed shop agreements, despite the TUC's declared opposition to this provision.

New policies, old attacks

In short, there has been a change in emphasis in Tory policy toward trade unions, although the object of these policies has remained the same. Increasingly, Tory policy has stressed the need to restructure trade unions as well as to control unions through restrictions on their behaviour. This change in emphasis emerged in the context of changing relations between labour and capital in the workplace. To this extent, it has been possible for the latest version of Tory policy to meet a 'populist' concern about trade union activity. The argument for union 'reform' has been presented in terms of the beleaguered and forgotten union member. Individual rights have been asserted over collective organization and activity. Similar appeals were ineffective at the time of the Heath government. In the early 1970s the trade union movement was relatively confident and prepared to claim that it could and would challenge state policy. Today, after the experience of the 'social contract' and the deepening crisis, unions are much more muted, in their activity and their claims. In such circumstances, it has been much easier for the government to develop policies based on a direct appeal to union members for change.

Recent Tory policy has focused on two specific areas of trade union organization: membership mobilization and trade union leadership. First, there is an attempt to undermine the basis of membership mobilization. In the past, it has been usual for the Conservative Party to argue that such proposals were necessary to lay the foundations for 'good' industrial relations. More recently, these arguments have been cast in the context of an overall programme for the economic recovery and prosperity of the nation. In the Conservative Party view, this requires weakening and demobilizing the trade union movement. A favoured recent alternative has been employer ballots, bypassing union structures altogether. This accords with a view that the state should not be directly involved in the conduct of disputes between workers and employers. Instead, the state should legislate to facilitate employers' control over workers. Second, there is an attempt to mould trade union leadership to the advantage of the government and employers. There has been an increasing emphasis in party statements on the desirability of postal ballots, especially for the election of national representatives. This view is based on an assessment that where postal ballots have been introduced they have resulted in the election of 'responsible' and cautious leaders. It is for this reason that ballot procedures have received attention in recent Tory pronouncements.

Thus there has been a new emphasis in the Tory commitment to legislate for the use of secret ballots in union elections and on issues involving industrial action. These proposals aim to weaken and demobilize unions, either by providing for the election of 'responsible' trade union leaders or by undermining the collective basis of union organization through the affirmation of the individual authority and responsibility of members. While there has been little disagreement about these aims, there has been an important shift in opinion about the way they can be achieved.

Labour Party: friend or foe?

The Labour Party approach to trade unions is premised on the assumption that there is a basic asymmetry between trade unions and employers in that trade unions are seen as the weaker partner in industry. Since the trade unions are regarded as the industrial wing of the labour movement, the Labour Party in office is presumed to work with the trade unions and sponsor legislation in their interest: e.g. the Trade Union and Labour Relations Act 1974 and 1976.

Despite this, there is considerable division within the Labour Party about trade union legislation in general, and ballot procedures in particular. There has been disagreement about the desirability of postal ballots for elections, strike ballots and whether legislation should make particular procedures compulsory. These disagreements partly reflect the difficulties of attempting to reconcile the party's 'partnership' with the trade unions with the 'efficient' management of the economy.

The Donovan Report and after

A useful starting point for understanding these apparently contradictory positions is the Donovan Report. This report was commissioned by the Labour government (1964–70) and, although an enquiry into trade unions and employers' organizations, it was concerned principally with trade unions. The commission sat from 1965 to 1968 and submitted its report to parliament in June 1968.

The report was critical of union procedures and practices and advocated that each trade union should set down in 'reasonable detail' the method of holding elections. However, the report was somewhat equivocal about recommending particular types of ballots. Postal ballots, for example, were seen as one way of increasing the levels of membership participation in elections, although it was noted that a majority of the membership still may not vote and that such ballots were relatively expensive. Using the example of the then Electrical Trades Union, Donovan claimed that compared with alternative procedures a higher level of participation in elections had been achieved with the postal ballot.

The Donovan Report reaffirmed the position of union leaders in the conduct of strikes. Compulsory ballots before strikes were rejected. In part, this was on the basis of evidence from North America which suggested that such ballots tended to result in strike action, rather than the reverse.

Following Donovan the Labour government published a White Paper, *In Place of Strife*. Although no reference was made to elections, strike ballots were advocated in some circumstances. It was envisaged that the Secretary of State should have a right to discuss with unions the desirability of holding a ballot of members or to consult with members when a 'major official strike' was imminent, unless there were 'valid reasons why a ballot or consultation should not take place'. Provision was also made for ballots on the question of strike action. The Secretary of State was to approve the form of the question to be put to the members but the ballot was to be conducted by the union and in accordance with its own rules.

Following union opposition to the White Paper and, perhaps more importantly, union opposition to the subsequent Conservative Industrial Relations Act 1971 the Labour Party did not legislate on strike ballots. In the Trade Union and Labour Relations Act 1974 the only reference to ballots was with regard to the requirement that trade unions should specify the procedure for elections or ballots. There was, however, reference to ballots in the Employment Protection Act 1975 with regard to union recognition, although this was not opposed by TUC unions. Indeed, in a period when the Labour government relied on trade union support and co-operation to implement key elements of its programme, particularly incomes policies, the government was inhibited from making proposals which many unions might oppose.

Divisions within the Labour Party

Nevertheless, within the Labour Party an influential view has often been expressed in favour of legislation on elections. In early May 1975, the Labour government accepted the principle of postal ballots for elections. Following backbench pressure from within the party, the government agreed to consult with the TUC about the possibility of state finance for trade union postal ballots. The TUC, wishing to distance itself from such a proposal, did not respond to this invitation. But the matter did not rest there, and was brought into sharp focus in late May 1975 when a number of backbench Labour members of parliament tabled an Early Day Motion advocating financial aid for postal ballots in elections. Such motions are presented to enable views to be expressed and to test opinion in the House through the addition of as many signatories as possible. Over a three-week period, 96 Labour Party members signed the motion. In addition, the Prime Minister declared himself in favour of postal ballots for trade union elections.

The reason for this motion was twofold. Most immediately, it was a response to the decision by the Amalgamated Union of Engineering Workers – Engineering Section, AUEW(ES), to abandon postal ballots for elections in the union (although this decision was declared invalid by the courts). It also complemented an unsuccessful Conservative Party amendment to the Employment Protection Bill to allow for free postal facilities for trade union elections. The motion was also seen by a number of the signatories as a contribution to the developing 'social contract' ethos of the time. Financial support for postal ballots was regarded as part of a process of strengthening trade union organization and thereby helping to develop a more constructive relationship between the Labour government and the trade union movement.

Equally, there has always been a section of the Labour Party which has been in favour of union autonomy over ballot procedures and the like. This was also evident at the time of the Early Day Motion just mentioned when an amendment affirming union autonomy in deciding union rules for elections was proposed and eventually signed by 54 Labour members of parliament.

Union autonomy

Subsequently, and in contrast to the Conservative Party, attention within the Labour Party focused on the use of ballots in the course of industrial action. In this respect, two issues were often conflated: the problem of union action which did not accord with the Labour government's policies (particularly on incomes) and the problem of legislation to enforce a change in trade union procedures. This was especially evident towards the end of Labour's term of office when pent-up frustrations exploded in the so-called 'winter of discontent' (1978–79). For instance, in November 1978, James Callaghan, who was then Labour Prime Minister, expressed dissatisfaction with mass meetings of union members to decide strike action. In line with the social contract ethos he affirmed that legislation on the activities of trade unions should only be introduced with the agreement of the unions. However, he also alluded to the possibility that sections of the trade union movement, perhaps the TUC, might be willing to consider a change in voting procedures so that the mass meeting would no longer be the principal way of deciding the progress of disputes.

These views were also evident in the formal agreement between the Labour government and the TUC, *The Economy, The Government and Trade Union Responsibilities*, published in 1979. Following a restatement of the 'social contract' between the Labour government and the TUC, covering industrial relations, industrial and technological change, and an assessment of the economy, this joint statement specified a 'code of conduct' for the duration of the 'social contract'. This code included a set of guidelines for negotiations and disputes procedures, strikes and picketing, and the maintenance of emergency services. In particular, the General Council of the TUC recommended that unions incorporate a set of principles covering strike ballots in their rules. While the form of the ballot was not specified, there was a clear recommendation in favour of strike ballots. This was one attempt to deal with the thorny problem for the Labour government of national strikes, particularly of the type that occurred during the 'winter of discontent'.

Concern was still being expressed about the procedures for electing union officials. Early in 1979 Harold Walker, Minister of State, Department of Employment, declared himself in favour of postal ballots for elections of trade union officials as well as in favour of strike ballots. Whilst endorsing Callaghan's caution against imposing such ballots under law, he reiterated the view that the Labour government would sympathetically consider union proposals for financial assistance to conduct membership ballots.

These different trends in the Labour Party are perhaps best illustrated in the Committee debate in the House of Lords over the 1980 Employment Bill. Then a number of influential Labour peers opposed the provision of public funds for secret ballots. In their opposition they referred to organizational problems and difficulties, as well as noting the desirability of mass meetings. Even so, this was not an objection to ballots as such, but rather to the element of compulsion in legislation. In this respect, the prevalent Labour Party view was simply reaffirmed.

Thus, within the Labour Party there have been longstanding divisions over policies towards unions in general and ballot procedures in particular. One section has always been in favour of legislation to introduce secret postal ballots for elections and possibly strikes. Another has been in favour of secret postal ballots but has been much more circumspect about legislating for their introduction. Yet a further section has always argued in favour of union autonomy over ballot procedures and the like. Clearly, these divisions have made it difficult for the Labour

Party to formulate a consistent and coherent set of policies toward the trade unions, at least on these issues.

Changing policies
There have also been important shifts in the emphasis of Labour Party policies toward trade unions over the last 15 years. At the time of the Donovan Report the prevalent view was in favour of union autonomy over ballot procedures for elections. There was, however, uncertainty about strike ballots, with the Labour government itself in favour of state intervention in major official strikes. Nevertheless, a more cautious view was adopted after the Tory experience with the Industrial Relations Act 1971 and the railways dispute in 1972. Subsequent legislation proposed by the Labour Party did not contain references to strike ballots. All the same, in 1979 the Labour government, in conjunction with the TUC, declared itself in favour of such ballots.

Advocacy of postal ballots has a more limited history. As already mentioned the principle of postal ballots for elections was accepted by the Labour government in 1975. But while declarations were made, legislation was not proposed. Instead, attention was focused on the relations between the Labour Party and the trade union movement.

After the election of a Conservative government in 1979, there was a further shift in policy. The different sections of the party have united against the threat of legal compulsion and there has been renewed emphasis on the value of union autonomy with regard to elections and strike ballots. The view has been expressed that unions should decide their rules and requirements themselves.

These twists and turns indicate the dilemma faced by the Labour Party. On the one hand, the party relies on trade union support for its policies and programmes. Such support is likely to be more forthcoming when union autonomy is recognized and affirmed. On the other hand, Labour government policies and programmes are often predicated on union restraint, particularly on pay issues. In these circumstances there has always been a strong impetus to strengthen national union leaders, through policies of incorporation and through reinforcing their position within union hierarchies; the corollary of this has been to consider ways of restricting workplace union autonomy. This has often led sections of the Labour Party to consider ways of encouraging the election of union leaders supportive of Labour Party policy. As a result, there has been no consistent development of policies toward unions in the Labour Party.

The Alliance: an old deal

The most wide-ranging set of proposals for the compulsory introduction of secret postal ballots have been advanced by the SDP. Following the founding of the party in 1981, a trade union reform policy group very quickly made trade union 'reform' the key to party policy on industrial relations. In two policy documents, *Reforming the Trade Unions* and *Industrial Relations, 1: Trade Union Reform*, the SDP advocated the introduction of secret postal ballots for elections of union executives and general secretaries as well as provision for the use of secret ballots to decide issues of industrial action. Alongside these papers, John Roper, SDP member of parliament, introduced a private members' bill in December 1982. It covered the use of secret postal ballots, periods of office, and conditions for election or appointment of general secretaries. These proposals were presented as part of a strategy for comprehensive industrial relations 'reform' which also included proposals for incomes policies and industrial democracy.

Giving unions back to members

Two principal reasons were advanced for these proposals. First, unions need to be 'reformed' to enable them to deal with current industrial problems and, second, archaic union structures have resulted in union councils dominated by politically left activists. The notion of 'archaic structures' provides the SDP with its rationale for 'reform', namely, as the document *Industrial Relations* put it: 'to return the trade unions to their members and restore their representativeness'.

This will be achieved by making secret postal ballots mandatory in elections for all executives and for those general secretaries who are elected rather than appointed. It is also argued that members should be able to 'trigger' ballots on industrial action. Following on from this, recommendations are made for ballot procedures and periods of election.

The second major set of recommendations dealt with referendums in unions. Having noted that referendums were used by unions on policy issues and rule changes before the 1920s, the papers declared in their favour. A number of reasons were advanced for this proposal. It was noted that there may be difficulties in drafting a law to cover the 'triggering' of a referendum and the appeals procedure. A 'more weighty objection' was that referendums may be used in 'frivolous and opportunist' ways by political opponents of union leaders. For these reasons, the papers included a recommendation that 'the right to trigger a ballot' be restricted to strikes and other forms of major industrial action. In the event that a strike call only involved a section of the membership then the ballot would be restricted to those members, although the decision would be binding on the union executive.

Thus the SDP has advanced a set of proposals to restructure trade unions through the introduction of secret postal ballots for elections and the widespread use of referendums. These proposals have been advanced on the assumption that it is necessary to legislate a membership role in union activity, and that through this trade union leadership will be made more 'representative' of that membership. In short, the claim for secret postal ballots was made in terms of democracy and a belief that through postal ballots members would elect moderate and cautious leaders.

In addition to the proposals about ballots, the SDP advocated other 'reforms' of unions. These included proposals to contract-in to the political levy, tax exemption for union contributions, assistance with union mergers, statutory rights for union recognition, a ban on pre-entry closed shops, the legal enforcement of procedure agreements, and of arbitration, and restrictions on secondary action and picketing.

Industrial partnership

While the SDP has produced a comprehensive programme for trade union reorganization, the Liberal Party, has made only fleeting reference to union ballots in its policy statements. All the same, the Liberal Party is committed to encourage the widest possible use of secret ballots in internal union elections and decision-making. This was evident in an Early Day Motion submitted in November 1975 by six leading Liberal Party members of parliament, advocating postal ballots for union elections. With reference to the increase in voting turnout in the AUEW(ES) following the introduction of postal ballots (from 5–11 per cent in 1972 to 27–55 per cent in 1975) the Liberal Party advocated such ballots as a means of achieving high levels of membership participation in union elections generally.

This view of trade unions, like that of the SDP, is premised on an assumption that the relations between workers and employers 'should' be that of partners rather than antagonists. Attention is focused on employee rights and industrial partnership and, as part of this, the Liberal Party claims that trade unions must be 'reformed' in order to achieve the maximum involvement of members in union affairs. This, it is suggested, would provide the basis for 'responsible' unions which would enter into 'constructive' relationships with employers and managers.

In developing its policy, the SDP drew on programmes developed within the Labour Party. As noted above, one section of the Labour Party has had a longstanding commitment to postal ballots for elections and strike ballots. Usually this view has been presented in terms of the rights of individual members, particularly with reference to participation. With the founding of the SDP, this became the centrepiece of the party's programme for industrial relations 'reform'.

The Alliance and the Trade Union Bill
As part of these commitments to 'reform' trade unions, the Alliance parties supported the Bill at its second reading, although this was not without reservation. The SDP welcomed the Bill but criticized it for not going far enough. Ian Wrigglesworth, the SDP spokesperson, expressed reservations that the Bill was not even-handed (on political levies), that the procedures for ballots should be extended (on the basis of one member one vote), and that the Bill was too narrow, with no mention of unofficial strikes or industrial democracy. For the Liberals, David Penhaligon regretted that the Bill did not take steps toward the industrial partnership 'dreamt' of by Liberals. Nonetheless, he welcomed the proposals on secret ballots for elections: he cautiously supported the proposals on political funds, and he expressed worries about the strike ballot provisions. Even so, the Liberal reservation was about the practicability of the proposals on strike ballots rather than the principle of those proposals. To an important extent, the Alliance parties simply differentiated themselves from the Tories on specifics while accepting the central tenets of the legislation.

The quest for 'reform'

Various proposals have been advanced by all major political parties on the basis that union 'reform' is desirable, if not necessary. For the Conservative Party and the Alliance, two assumptions have been made:

there are problems with trade union organization and structure which should be evident to everyone, not least the members;
the state has the right and duty to be concerned with union 'reform', if not to impose change on unions.

Following on from this, debate has often been concerned with the degree to which compulsion for change is necessary or even desirable.

In the course of developing these arguments it has been common to link two questions: First, should ballots be conducted in secret? And second, should postal ballots be introduced for union elections? Often this has led to a shift in the arguments about 'reform', from a consideration of the practical problems faced by unions to a general consideration of union democracy. Frequently, claims have been made on behalf of particular practices on the grounds that by definition they are more democratic than others. It is as if the claim that a particular procedure is democratic is sufficient justification for any particular policy.

Even the Labour Party, which because of its historical links with the trade union movement should be able to propose a policy affirming the principles of union democracy, has ended up advocating what are in fact anti-democratic procedures and practices. Nevertheless, it must be noted that the proposals made by the Labour Party have been viewed as strengthening the unions by proposing reforms which would affirm 'responsible' strongly led unions. This has been complemented by proposals to restrict workplace union autonomy. Consequently, this sometimes has led the Labour Party to advocate proposals which would undermine collective organization, such as postal ballots. So for the Labour Party, too, despite its historical links with the trade unions, the demands of government are such that the imperative to control and curtail certain types of union activity holds sway.

In order to give a clearer idea of the different views of various parties, it is necessary to clarify the different definitions which have been applied to 'union democracy'. It is to this that I turn in the following chapter.

3. Definitions of Union Democracy

This chapter examines the two major definitions of union democracy and considers the way in which questions of union democracy have been taken up by politicians and union leaders, particularly the TUC. The chapter begins by detailing the principles of union democracy as I understand them, namely organization and activities distinguished by collective membership participation and involvement. Against this, the most common view of union democracy is one which holds that particular aspects of parliamentary democracy are most suitable for unions, and as such is an argument for individualism and a rejection of the view that unions can be vehicles for socialist struggle. This is then followed by a consideration of the ways these views on union democracy have been taken up by politicians and union leaders.

Union democracy

In my view any notion of union democracy worthy of the name should be about membership participation and decision-making. Such involvement and participation is the essential ingredient for the vitality and success of unions. From this perspective the formal features of democratic union life are the processes of meetings, mandating and advising delegates, receiving reports back, and determining policies and union activities, such as support for campaigns and how best to pursue the implementation of union policy. Informally, such a democracy is signified by dialogue between members and their delegates, particularly work groups and their stewards, but also at all other levels of the union. Union democracy is thus a continuous process rooted in the daily experience of most workers and involving a continuous struggle about the conditions of employment, the authority of employers and the organization of work. On this basis union democracy is founded on the continual interaction between workers and their delegates.

Disagreement and discussion, argument and counter-argument, are the key features of this process – a sign of the vitality and indeed the essence of union organization. The reason for this is that the experience of members is often varied and there are not always obvious and clear-cut ways to proceed and advance the interests of the membership. Through meetings, discussions and debate, decisions are made and policy formulated; through discussion and careful consideration of candidates, delegates are elected or encouraged to stand for office. And, of course, decisions should be, and often are, opened up for further consideration and decision. Examination and re-examination of policy, consideration and reconsideration of delegates, are the essential features of this view of democracy. In this way collective interests (rather than individual preference) are expressed and made manifest.

Delegation rather than representation should therefore be a key feature of union organization. The delegate is accountable to and controlled by members. Policy is decided at meetings and conferences. Local and national delegates are then instructed to put these decisions into practice. At times this may involve speaking and acting on behalf of members in negotiations, in meetings with employers, politicians and so on. But, and decisively, any decision or agreement must be subject to ratification by members following debate and discussion on delegates' reports. Only then is democracy realized.

This form of democracy is associated with a view of structure and organization which enables members to have popular control of delegates and the union apparatus. It is a view of democracy which sees participation and involvement by members as the key feature. Thus, members are actively involved in the formulation of union policy, in the process of collective bargaining, in the control of delegates and officials, and in the organization and activity of the union.

As such, the union is characterized by a continuous dialogue between members and delegates aimed at developing policy and organizing union activity. The purpose of elections is to elect those most likely to accept the responsibilities of delegates through a process of continuous accountability. For their part, delegates are obliged to debate strategy and tactics, and policy and progress, with members, and to be answerable to them.

Much of this might appear unexceptionable and it is sobering to realize that this form of participatory democracy is seldom achieved. Such a view of democracy has been argued for by many active members who have experienced the benefits and strength of participation. It is a view of democracy which has occasionally met with a rhetorical response by some left-wing sections of the trade union hierarchies. But it is a view which has seldom been put into practice.

Parliamentary union democracy

The most common view of union democracy is one modelled on parliamentary democracy and taking some very particular features from it. One common focus is on ballot procedures. Central to this is the notion that the rights of the individual member should be recognized and sanctified through particular ballot procedures. Three elements are stressed as democratic principles furthered by this approach:

> it is the right of members that one person has one vote, that votes are cast in secret and that representatives rather than delegates are elected at periodic intervals;
> a truly democratic union is one that is organised so that all members can mark a ballot paper;
> the only way to ascertain members' views is to add up all the votes cast.

In this way democracy is defined with reference to ballot procedures. Put baldly, voting equals secret individual ballots equals democracy. More specifically, democracy is often associated with a particular ballot procedure, namely postal ballots, and this is often elevated into a central aspect of democratic practice.

Another variant of this general approach emphasises the representative structures of unions. It is argued that there is no single form of representative democracy. There are many forms, just as there are many forms of parliamentary democracy. The people of Great Britain, France and the United States of America, for example, elect parliamentary representatives and decide policy according to different procedures. So, in this view, postal ballots, voting at work and voting at branch meetings are all democratic procedures. At most, practical demands may decide a preference for one procedure rather than another.

In these views of representative union democracy, control and representation are specified in particular ways:

> control of leaders by members some of the time, namely at elections or conferences;
> the sovereignty of representatives between elections, namely the right of elected (and appointed) leaders to represent members without direct reference to them.

The argument for union democracy in this version is presented in terms of two aspects of parliamentary democracy: procedure and representation. Not surprisingly, it is these two aspects which are stressed by the major political parties in their proposals for union reform. More surprising is the fact that this is also the view of democracy which is usually advanced, not just by the main political parties, but also in official union policies.

The major political parties and union democracy

As detailed in Chapter 2, proposals to 'reform' unions have been advanced by all mainstream parties in Britain. By pointing to particular examples of bad practice it has been argued that the state should intervene to reorganize unions. Usually this is justified in the name of democracy.

In general, two models of 'democratic reform' have been put forward. One entails proposals for what is claimed to be a 'constructive' relationship between unions and workers by creating the conditions for centralized authoritative union leaderships able to work with governments. This view predominates within the Labour Party. So, 'democratic reform' has been advanced as a way of creating responsible unions able to participate in collective bargaining structures in a 'constructive' manner. In this way the first tentative parliamentary steps can be taken to transform a capitalist economy to a socialist one.

The intention of the other model of 'democratic reform', advanced by the Conservative Party, is to weaken and demobilize unions. The aim of this view is to produce unions concerned with only a narrow range of issues, and with limited opportunities to strike or engage in similar types of industrial action. It is seen as an 'orderly' way to redress the balance between workers and employers, since as everyone knows, 'unions are too powerful'. In this way the capitalist economy will be protected and indeed strengthened.

In this context reform has been presented as a means of making union leadership more responsive to members through the establishment of alternative decision-making structures and procedures. This generally takes the form of advocating the establishment of new structures and procedures, preferably postal ballots, but also secret individual ballots, which should complement if not replace current arrangements, such as a sovereign conference. The classic case referred to by advocates of this position is the procedure for making strike decisions. On the one hand, it is often argued that decisions are taken by unrepresentative conferences called for this purpose; on the other hand, it is claimed that postal ballots or secret individual ballots of the members concerned would give a clear picture of the degree of support for the action. To this extent these ballots are seen as a means of extending democratic practice in unions.

In general, these arguments have been presented in very sweeping terms. It has often been claimed that unions are controlled and manipulated by unrepresentative and undemocratic leaderships. At the same time it is often argued that union procedures open up the possibility of outside interference or demagogic control of the ordinary members. So what is to be done? Increasingly it has been asserted that particular procedures, usually based on a vague comparison with parliamentary procedures, are the panacea for these problems.

TUC rhetoric, union practice

Unions are committed to union democracy. As an indication of this, the question of union democracy has been a constant source of friction within the movement. The problem is that the debate has often been channelled into a concern with particular constitutional procedures, with the result that democracy as process has been overlooked and ignored. To illustrate, there have been gales of rhetoric in defence of or in opposition to the re-election of officials every five years. However, this issue is only one of many and is by no means the most important. Indeed, I shall now argue, a concern with the vitality and circumstances of workplace union organization is much more important.

In part, the channelling of debate toward specific constitutional procedures has its basis in the claim that unions are largely democratic in the procedures for decision-making and the forms of representation. This has enabled the TUC in particular to assert that unions are committed to union democracy, as evidenced in union policy and practice.

TUC leaders have pointed to a variety of election procedures as indicators of democratic practice. These procedures range from postal ballots, to secret ballots at meetings, to votes by a show of hands. Constituencies include the entire membership, meetings of small groups or sections of members in workplaces, branches, trade or industrial sections, and conferences.

Similar claims are made about procedures for decision-making, which are also very varied. They include procedures for determining policy and industrial action. In addition, many executive committees have considerable discretion over the implementation of policy and, indeed, over the means of authorizing various forms of industrial action. At the same time there is evidence that some unions are bound in rule to refer key decisions on pay and related matters to the membership for ratification, either at special conferences, branch meetings or membership ballots.

In almost every British union the annual or biennial conference is the sovereign policy-making body. Usually conference delegates are mandated on some matters, able to exercise discretion on others. Between conferences decisions are interpreted, implemented and dealt with by executive committees. There is often considerable discretion for an executive committee to vary, reconsider or to ignore a conference decision.

While individual unions have made claims that these different practices are democratic, it is the TUC which has spoken on behalf of trade unions in general. As already mentioned, the TUC saw fit to commit itself in the 1979 agreement with the then Labour government to the principle of strike ballots. More than this, the procedures agreed to by the TUC incorporated many of the principles associated with parliamentary democracy rather than union democracy. This included a recommendation to unions that they take steps to provide for the use of individual membership ballots in strike ballots.

This preference for a version of parliamentary democracy has also been evident in the campaigns against the Trade Union Bill and associated papers. Before revealing this preference the TUC often begins with a claim that all TUC unions are basically democratic, as was the case in the recent TUC publication *Hands Up for Union Democracy* where the claim was made that: 'Just as there are many different unions so there are many different forms of union democracy.' So, it is claimed: 'Every man and every woman who belongs to a trade union in Britain has a voice and a vote in their union's affairs.' This reiterates the view that union democracy can be expressed in many different ways, and that most of these are evident in British unions.

The TUC would appear to be a firm adherent to the principle of union autonomy. On this issue, the TUC view is that where 'reform' is necessary the relevant unions will make the appropriate changes. In support of the principle of union autonomy the TUC is able to point to a long history of legislative interference in trade union affairs and practice which has restricted and hindered unions. And, of course, the current legislation on trade unions was presented to parliament in exactly these terms.

More recently, however, the TUC has felt compelled to defend the principle of union autonomy with reference to specific unions, a particularly dangerous practice when there is no consensus about what constitutes union democracy. Specifically, the Inland Revenue Staff Federation (IRSF) was singled out as a union which was voluntarily considering the way it was organized with a view to introducing changes in line with the Tory government's legislation. In 1983 that union commissioned a firm of industrial relations consultants to study and report on the organization of the union. The package of recommendations based on the report, and placed before a delegate conference in December 1983, included proposals for pre-strike ballots and a national executive elected by individual ballots. While the membership survey conducted by the consultants indicated individual membership support for these proposals, the activist-dominated branch meetings which mandated delegates for the conference rejected the proposals, despite a letter sent by the general secretary, Tony Christopher, and the president, Clive Boote, to all members urging them to attend branch meetings and support the executive proposals. Christopher stated: 'If we do not make these reforms we will be giving the lie to Mr Len Murray's statement that trade unions can deal with their own democracy. The 1984 Act will require us to turn our attention to this.' In the event, the delegate conference agreed a mixed bag of proposals: secret membership ballots for the election of president, vice presidents, executive committee, office chairperson and secretary, and to confirm the appointment of future general secretaries. It rejected secret membership ballots before strikes and for the election of branch committees.

The difficulty for the TUC was that the initiative by the IRSF Executive had been specifically mentioned in the TUC campaign against the Tory government's legislation on union 'reform'. The decision by the IRSF on strike ballots was seen as a blow to the TUC attempt to demonstrate to the government that unions were capable of changing themselves in ways favoured by the Tories. In this context the IRSF conference decision should be welcomed since the union did not agree to introduce procedures for strike decision-making which would further isolate and individualize the membership. Instead, sections of the membership defended the principles of collective organization, for example by arguing for area mass meetings for the consideration of industrial action and claiming that such meetings ensured 'an informed and democratic debate where all aspects of the question at hand can be brought to members' attention'. This example serves to underline the fundamental weakness of the TUC position, supported, of course, by many individual unions, that not only can unions 'reform' themselves but they *will* 'reform' themselves in line with Tory wishes. More than this, it shows the way in which the TUC and many union leaderships have a partiality for the type of 'reforms' advocated by the Conservative Party and, in the past, by sections of the Labour Party. In short, it reveals the commitment among many official union leaders to versions of parliamentary democracy.

Nevertheless, there have been major debates in some unions about the most appropriate way to elect representatives; for instance in the Civil and Public Services' Association (CPSA) and in the AUEW(ES). A number of unions have undertaken studies of their organization to see whether current procedures are most appropriate for current conditions (NUPE and the SCPS). This occasionally has resulted in major reorganization and changes in practice, often in the name of democracy. In other unions, proposals to reorganize have met with negative responses and occasionally have resulted in the censure of the proponents of change (a common occurrence in the Electrical, Electronic, Telecommunication and Plumbing Union: EETPU).

Thus, there is great variation in procedure and practice. When criticism is raised, the usual response has been to make a virtue out of variation, all in the name of democracy. This, to an important extent, has meant ignoring and overlooking the very real defects within existing unions. This is a dangerous oversight; it means that the critics of unions have often been able to pose in coats of many democratic colours, ignoring the degree to which current union practice is really democratic or not. It has also meant that the link between union democracy and socialism has been ignored or even rejected.

4. Debates about Union Democracy

While the debate about union democracy has been cast in general terms, a number of specific issues have been highlighted as particular problems. These include voting procedures and membership participation and control. In this chapter the debates about these features of union organization will be reviewed.

Voting

One of the principal issues addressed in debates about union democracy is the procedures for elections and decision-making. These procedures may range from postal ballots and secret membership ballots to membership meetings and conferences. Each will be examined in turn.

Postal ballots
Increasingly it has been common for 'moderate' trade union leaders and right-wing politicians (including members of the Labour Party) to advocate the use of secret postal ballots. The argument in favour has been based on an assumption that unions should be organized as aggregates of individuals, each of whom can independently and autonomously indicate their concerns and preferences. It is claimed that unions increasingly negotiate in circumstances which do not necessarily require membership involvement. Indeed, it is sufficient to have procedures which provide a framework for the occasional involvement of members, indicating preferences about negotiating issues or considering support for industrial action.

It is further claimed that the introduction of secret postal ballots would result in more fully representative unions, by allowing all members' views to be taken into account. In this way organizational forms that allow the views of the activists or, more dangerously, the extremists, to predominate would be overcome. This, it is argued, would be the outcome of introducing proper democratic procedures and practices.

There are two main types of argument against the introduction of postal ballots: procedural and political. Procedural ones focus on practical problems along with the fact that they do not necessarily result in higher levels of participation. Political objections are premised on a view that unions are collective organizations rather than aggregates of individuals and that reliance on such procedures would weaken rather than strengthen unions.

In general most of the arguments against postal ballots have focused on the procedural level. The point has been made, correctly, that there are enormous practical problems relating to the organization and conduct of ballots, which often rely on a degree of organization beyond the resources of most unions. At the same time, these proposals often open up the possibility of extensive outside interference in the affairs of unions.

It has frequently been claimed that more cautious, responsible and conservative union leaders would be elected through postal ballots. While this is not necessarily the case (e.g. the Bakers Union, where in recent years left-wing leaders have often been elected through this system), in terms of the wider terrain of the debate, it is a side issue. More importantly the introduction of postal ballots is likely to give power without responsibility to the indifferent and uninvolved union member. Such members are often referred to as apathetic or part of the silent majority. More to the point, indifference and lack of involvement arises because members are unable to participate in the union. In such circumstances, the introduction of postal ballots would enable these members to have the appearance – but not the reality – of involvement in union governance.

Few arguments against postal ballots have been presented in terms of the view that unions are essentially collective organizations. Nevertheless, the essence of the argument is clear: the emphasis would be on the strength of collective organization and action, physically through meetings and ideologically through an affirmation of collective interests. In this respect, unions must provide for debate and discussion, dissension and agreement. This cannot be achieved through postal ballots. It can only be achieved where procedures enable agreement to be reached in a collective way, where union leaders are elected on the basis of collective consideration.

Individual membership ballots

In opposition to postal ballots, it is often argued that the individual membership ballot for elections and decision-making is a more authentically democratic procedure. The vote is still secret and it takes place at a membership meeting either at the workplace or at a branch meeting. As a result, one of the problems with postal ballots is overcome, in that members meet to discuss and debate issues or the appropriateness of candidates. Such a requirement may be an integral part of the individual membership ballot.

It is usual for such ballot procedures to be advocated for elections and key decisions. Such decisions usually include those about national industrial action (e.g. the NUM). Apart from this it is argued that the foundation and development of policy is best done at national delegate conferences where delegates from branches or areas can meet together and consider policy.

Where individual membership ballots are organized the usual procedure is for individual members to cast their vote in secret after listening to the debate. The votes are then counted up for the meeting and aggregated with votes cast at other meetings. In this way an aggregate vote is obtained for the relevant constituency.

It is often claimed that this procedure achieves the best of all worlds. First, meetings are held to debate and discuss the issue and ballots are conducted in secret. Second, only those prepared to vote are included in the final count. In this way the ballot is an accurate reflection of those who have participated and all members feel that their votes count. Third, as the membership becomes more involved, sees the value of debating and discussing an issue and casting a vote, then the union will develop in a more democratic direction, with broader and broader membership participation.

While an improvement on the total atomization of the constituency which the postal ballot is based on, the practice of casting votes in secret is still an individualizing act which does not accord well with the traditions of collective organization and actions. In this respect members attend a meeting, they listen, consider and participate in a collective discussion or debate. Then they cast their vote as individuals, in the privacy of a corner of the room or a cubicle, as if the meeting was no longer relevant. Indeed, the casting of the vote could well come to be regarded as more important than the meeting. In this circumstance the meeting may be truncated, non-contentious or simply suspended. In fact the very procedure which is designed to encourage debates and discussions paradoxically may result in reaffirming the individual and private act of the closet voter rather than the union member committed to collective organization and actions.

Membership meetings

Paradoxically, large-scale membership meetings are regarded by many as undemocratic. At such meetings all the relevant members gather together, debate and discuss the issue and then vote, usually by a show of hands. This is the meeting highlighted by the media. It is the meeting which is often held at a workplace to decide industrial action, to commence, continue or conclude industrial action. Occasionally, such meetings are held to consider a national pay offer (e.g. Ford Motor Co.).

It is often argued that such meetings are the antithesis of democratic procedures. This view was summarized in a recent government Green Paper, *Democracy in Trade Unions*: 'Few things have done more to lower public regard for trade unions than the spectacle of strike decisions being taken by a show of hands at stage-managed mass meetings to which outsiders may be admitted and where dissenters may be intimidated' (p. 17). In 1978 Labour Prime Minister James Callaghan also saw fit to cast doubt on the mass meeting as the most appropriate way to reach decisions about industrial action, although he was circumspect about his reason for thinking so.

In general there are two stated reasons for opposing large membership meetings: first, it is supposed that such meetings are open to outside non-union members, and second, it is believed that people are intimidated into voting against their better judgement. Obviously critics of such meetings have never attempted to go along themselves otherwise they would know that it is highly unlikely that non-union members could attend and vote even if they wished to. Such comments also betray a very arrogant and patronizing view of the average worker as a person who will be cowed by debate and discussion, as if debate and discussion were not the bread and butter of most working-class lives.

Supporters of the large-scale membership meetings point to it as a superior way of determining and deciding issues because these meetings are predicated on arguments, dissent and disagreement. In this respect they are a very sophisticated way of reaching a decision. In comparison the ballot, with its one question (which is highly susceptible to loaded wording), allows for none of the nuances that people may feel about the issue and is thus a very crude way of reaching a decision.

All the same, it is important not to idealize the mass meeting as the untainted exemplar of collective decision-making. Such meetings can be manipulated by a small coterie of people, through the conduct of the meeting, control of the agenda or the organization of the vote. In addition, mass meetings do not necessarily lend themselves to the easy amendment of resolutions and a detailed consideration of issues. Indeed, on occasion amendments may not even be accepted for debate and consideration. Even so, such problems can be best met through an informed and active membership which will encourage the development of good practice and guard against the dangers of manipulation and control.

It is also as well not to become blinded by the image of 10,000 workers gathered together in a field debating and deciding policy. This of course is only one type of membership meeting, although the most often publicized. In addition there are the numerous workshop and office membership meetings, occurring either at branch level or in the workplace. Such meetings involve the mass membership as much as the highly publicized and visible factory meeting. On such occasions action is decided, policy formulated and workplace leaders instructed on how to proceed. Indeed, in a real sense, the mass meeting, looked at in this broader perspective, can be seen as the basis of most union structures. When a union is grounded on such practice then the union is democratically alive and thriving. This meeting is surely the exemplar of union democracy rather than its antithesis.

The block vote
One further and related issue on elections and decision-making revolves around the manner of determining a branch vote. It is a feature of many unions that votes for policy and candidates for office are cast by means of a block vote. This means that irrespective of the number attending a branch meeting (or equivalent), or irrespective of the split in the vote to mandate conference delegates, the vote recorded at conference is the total membership of the branch (or equivalent).

The block vote procedure gives rise to the phenomenon of the card vote at conferences to settle disputed conference decisions. On such occasions delegates may vote by show of hands in the first instance. If this vote is challenged, a card vote is called and the very same delegates vote, but this time they record the total branch membership (or proportion thereof) as if all the members had been present and had cast their vote as the delegates did, or indeed as the members present at the original branch meeting had done.

The block vote procedure has been questioned as an undemocratic practice. It has been argued that this procedure gives the members attending meetings to decide policy an authority and discretion that is unwarranted and unjustified. In some circumstances it can lead to domination of conferences by relatively few large branches (or equivalent). In these circumstances it is often argued that a referendum would be a much more equitable way of deciding policy, at least on major questions.

Against this it must be said that all members have a constitutional right to attend meetings, decide policy and mandate delegates. As a result, it is reasonable for those who actually attend to decide branch policy – which after all is generally binding on all members – and cast votes accordingly. Such a procedure serves to reaffirm the collective base of union organization and should be recognized as such. Since policy is binding on all, it is reasonable to involve all members as if they had attended the relevant meetings.

The problem is that membership meetings are not always accessible to all for a variety of reasons. Members may not be able to attend membership meetings because of work patterns such as shift work, or other factors such as domestic responsibilities. Meetings may also appear unwelcoming. If the majority in attendance are men and you are a woman, if most members are white and you are black, then membership meetings can be hostile experiences. Where members are unable to attend meetings or feel inhibited from attending then the block vote procedure is genuinely undemocratic.

In short, the debates about postal ballots, individual membership ballots, membership meetings, and the block vote are cast in terms of debates about the procedures of democracy. These practices are regarded by their advocates as exemplars of democratic practice. To a large extent, recent debates have focused on these issues.

Membership participation and control

Debates about union democracy have a broader focus than voting procedures; they have also been concerned with forms of participation and control. This has given rise to debates about membership involvement, forms of representation and tendencies toward bureaucracy.

Meeting attendance and participation

One concern in the debates about union democracy has been the participation of members in union activity. In part, this concern arises from the assertion that the union is the members, thereby implying that if decisions and actions are taken in the name of the union, then members must be involved and their views clearly and faithfully represented. This requirement has been the focus of many debates about union democracy.

Increasingly, it is becoming recognized, as mentioned above, that many members face acute difficulties in participating in union activity. It is, of course, easiest for union members to participate at the workplace, but even so there still may be difficulties, for instance in the case of branch meetings held after hours and in inconvenient places which many members may be unable or reluctant to attend. In some unions, branches cover whole regions, thereby necessitating difficult travel arrangements to attend meetings. Even if meetings are seldom held, members must still make special efforts to attend. For many, the demands of family life, the absence of branch-organized creches or the difficulty of travel, especially in the evenings, may preclude attendance at meetings. These problems are aggravated where branches are not defined by workplace, and they often result in a separation between immediate workplace, and other issues. This may further inhibit attendance at branch meetings.

Another set of problems often referred to in this respect concerns the lack of workplace-based forms of representation in some unions, such as local stewards, particularly in the public sector. Where such structures are absent or minimally developed, members are not likely to participate in union activity because there is no structural basis for representation, meeting, debate or discussion. Under these circumstances it has been common for many to argue for the establishment of workplace-based representative structures.

Of course, when there is minimal participation some unionists and many opponents of trade unions have looked to postal ballots as a way of overcoming some of the problems. The introduction of postal ballots, it is claimed, would make it possible for members' views to be represented and expressed.

But might not such a solution merely aggravate the situation? Instead of encouraging participation in union activity, with its concomitants of discussion and debate, it could serve to fragment the union further. In these circumstances the disengagement of members from union organization and activity would be confirmed rather than overcome. Any real solution to what is after all a real problem must depend on facing up to the need to reduce the barriers to members attending meetings by a variety of means, rather than doing away with meetings altogether.

Accountability and control

The other side of non-involvement is accountability. The argument about accountability is that representatives should be truly accountable through elections as well as for decisions taken. If they are not, then they are likely to be out of touch with members or may even be prone to manipulate members in favour of particular policies.

With regard to elections, it is often claimed that particular procedures (e.g. postal ballots) offer the only way of making representatives truly accountable. This argument may be extended to include recommendations in favour of election addresses, report backs and so on. In this way, it is argued, representatives would be forced to present themselves to the whole membership (or relevant constituency) to defend a stand and justify their policies and record.

It has also been argued that referendums on policy issues and strikes are an important form of accountability in unions, and procedures such as postal ballots the most appropriate form of ballot for these. In this way policies, particularly about national strikes and pay offers, could be subject to the consideration of the whole membership, resulting, it is claimed, in policies supported by the whole membership. Furthermore, runs the argument, such procedures would break the stranglehold of small cohesive sections of membership who dominate because they are not accountable to the membership. By providing for greater participation and accountability, it is claimed, the views of the whole membership would prevail.

What is at stake, once again, is what is meant by union democracy. I would claim, in opposition to the above line of argument, that an authentic form of accountability and control can arise only in the context of collective organization and action. From this point of view then, accountability and control become a process of reports and recommendations, argument, collective consideration and decision. Through mass meetings in the workplace or at conferences covering a section of the membership, a region or the whole membership, decisions are made and representatives elected. Disagreement and discussion, argument and counter-argument, are the key features of this process. This is because the experience of members is often varied and there is not always an obvious way to proceed and advance the interests of the membership.

And, of course, in such a process decisions should be and often are opened up again for further consideration and decision. Examination and re-examination of policy, consideration and reconsideration of union representatives are the essential features of collective organization and activity. In this way, accountability and control become an integral part of collective organization and action.

Representatives and delegates

One of the issues which has not been subject to recent debate but which unions debated in the past is that of representation or delegation. Briefly, representation occurs when the rights and preferences of members are considered but are not regarded as binding on elected representatives or in the course of negotiations and the conduct of industrial and political action. Delegation, in contrast, refers to popular control over policy and elected officials by the membership.

These represent two forms of accountability and signify two views of democracy: the first based on the principle of servicing the membership; the latter based on membership control. It has been argued that servicing the membership means that a union is organized on the basis of a shrewd and sensitive leadership, a body of officials who owe their position to their knowledge and expertise, and maintain a steady downward flow of communication and information to the members. In such a union the membership at large have very little responsibility for the active development and pursuit of the unions' policies and objectives, nor would they see any virtue in such involvement.

The case of delegation has been presented as the recognition that the principle of participation should underpin a union's organization and pursuit of policies. In such unions, the emphasis is on the active involvement of members in the development of policy, the process of collective bargaining, the conduct of industrial and political action, and the control of representatives and officials. Communication would be an inherently two-way process, embracing a continuous dialogue between all members at all levels. Those who are elected to office or who speak on behalf of membership would have been chosen because they would accept the responsibility of representation through a system of continuous accountability and control by the membership. In such a union, there would be the opportunity for sustained debate about strategy and tactics involving the membership of all levels. Indeed this would be seen as essential to the life and fortunes of the union.

Elections or appointment
Alongside representation and delegation concern has often been expressed about the election or appointment of full-time paid officials. The issue basically is whether such officials should be elected by some membership constituency or whether they should be appointed, usually by an executive committee (although often subject to ratification by conference).

As noted above there has been a longstanding practice in many unions, mainly the manual unions in the private sector, of electing at least the senior officials of the unions. In contrast, relatively few senior officials are elected in unions recruiting white-collar workers. Obviously this difference in practice is buried in past union experiences and traditions.

Recently the argument has been presented by the Tories and the SDP that appointment, particularly of general secretaries, is appropriate where such officials do not have a vote on union governing bodies. More than this, it is argued that some unions, particularly white-collar unions, should seek a general secretary and associated officials who have expertise and experience which are valuable to the union. Under such circumstances it would be inappropriate to elect such officials.

But why should full-time paid officials not be subject to the same processes as all other leaders of the union, namely periodic election? It is only when officials are elected that they will be genuinely accountable to the membership and indeed genuinely represent the membership. When elected officials must report back to members, give an account of their stewardship and subject themselves to recall and re-election. This is surely a condition for an authentically democratic union.

Bureaucracy or democracy

At the most general level, there has been a longstanding debate about the character of trade unionism in advanced capitalist societies. Some argue that bureaucracy is an inevitable feature of modern unions. Others counter by claiming that any discernible trends towards bureaucracy are not inevitable and, indeed, democratic unionism is not only possible but should be achieved.

Perhaps the most influential argument has been that which sees a compulsion in unions toward bureaucracy. To be more specific, it is argued, following Robert Michels's classic pre-First World War study *Political Parties*, that there is an imperative in large mass organizations like unions such that 'who says organization says oligarchy'. In other words irrespective of the origins of different unions, a layer of influential full-time persons will appear, relatively removed from and unaccountable to the membership: they will be in a position to make or at least influence the key decisions and policies of the union. In addition, and partly as a corollary of this development a relatively sophisticated division of labour will emerge so as to more effectively pursue the objectives of the union but which, in fact, will serve to reinforce the trends toward oligarchy in particular and bureaucracy in general.

This general proposition has been extended by some to argue that the process of bureaucratization has become a feature of *all* levels of union structure and organization. In particular, it has been argued that at the level of the workplace, with the advent of check-off arrangements, the extension of facility provisions and the drawing of senior workplace representatives into consultations with local management, this layer of representatives has become removed and separated from the membership.

Indeed, this argument can be extended to become the justification for democracy by procedure. Specifically, it is claimed that through the introduction of particular ballot procedures (like postal ballots) the union will be returned to the membership and thereby become more democratic.

But surely this misses the point. While unions have become bureaucratized and thus have become seduced by the appeal of collaboration with employers, they still remain collective organizations which are the foundation for democratic participation and involvement. For this to develop, the trends toward bureaucracy need to be countered by union structures based on direct democracy. Examples of such organization are to be found, for instance, in the development of workplace union branches where stewards are democratically accountable. In this way, democracy can be enhanced through the participation and involvement of union members at the workplace and hence throughout the union.

This means that it is necessary for trade unionists to recognize that there are very real pressures toward oligarchy, bureaucratization and class collaboration. Such pressures arise in the context of the changing contours of contemporary capitalist society. This, however, does not mean that these pressures are inevitable or irresistible. The task, surely, is to oppose and resist such developments. In this it must be acknowledged that some organizational forms can help and others hinder moves toward democratic trade unionism. But ultimately there is no substitute for a committed, aware and active membership. This is the cornerstone of union democracy.

Thus the issue of bureaucracy is about the possibility of union democracy. With this in mind, the question is: how best can unions be structured so that members' interests can be expressed and recognized. For advocates of a participatory form of democracy this requires that unions be concerned with the means by which members are able to participate and become involved in union activity. Accountability, then, means engagement with all members, reporting back, seeking guidance, developing arguments and considering alternatives. Only then will an authentic union democracy develop where the membership control and decide their futures. This is the issue facing trade unionists.

Many issues have been addressed in these debates about union democracy, ranging from concerns about specific procedures to general questions about the organization of power in unions. But, as I have argued, the benchmark for judging these features of union organization and operation must be with reference to the conditions for membership participation, collective organization and action. It is therefore worth while and necessary to take a closer look at the degree to which union practice is democratic or not. In the next three chapters I shall look in turn at ballot procedures, forms of representation and links between unions and 'politics'.

5. Many Ways to Ballot the Membership

The aim of this chapter is to identify and specify some of the variations in union ballots and the circumstances which have given rise to these variations. In so doing it will become evident that many of the debates about union democracy have been premised on simplistic generalizations about union organization and activity.

The incidence of ballots

Ballots in some shape or form are a feature of all union organization. Unions almost always elect their national executives, although the procedures vary from secret postal ballots to delegate conference ballots. Less common is the membership election of general secretaries (and other full-time officials). Alongside these ballots, a number of unions have provisions for ballots to consider the commencement, continuation, or conclusion of major industrial action, and more commonly to consider annual pay offers. Again ballots may range from secret postal ballots to delegate conference ballots. In some unions this includes longstanding provisions for ballots at membership meetings by a show of hands.

There is enormous variation in union ballot procedures. No single pattern is evident, either in election methods or the methods of selecting general secretaries. This variation is the consequence of the different histories, traditions and peculiar problems of unions. To give a full account of this, beyond the simplistic generalizations of party programmes, would necessitate a consideration of the nature and character of work organization; the divisions between men and women, manual and non-manual, skilled and unskilled workers; the political traditions of the union; and the changing patterns of employment.

More than this, it should be noted that unions have not been complacent about their methods of organization. As the Labour Research Department report, *Our Unions, Our Democracy*, reveals, 10 of the 26 largest TUC unions have changed their procedures in the last decade, and a further 6 have debated changes in the same period. Clearly, reorganization with regard to ballot procedures is a concern of many unions.

Five unions

With regard to ballots, there is considerable variation in voting procedures, even within the general category of membership ballots. This variation can be illustrated by a brief consideration of the procedures used by five different unions.

AUEW(ES)

The Amalgamated Union of Engineering Workers: Engineering Section: all officers, from district secretaries to the president and general secretary, are elected by postal ballot. In these ballots, head office under the direction of the general secretary addresses and posts ballot forms to the members at their home addresses. When completed the ballot forms are posted by pre-paid envelopes back to head office. The forms are then counted at the head office under the scrutiny of tellers appointed by the executive committee. Candidates are entitled to submit election addresses which are available at branch offices for interested members to read. In contrast, shop stewards may be elected by workers in each workplace by show of hands or by other ballot procedures, although once elected the stewards are subject to approval by local district committees. With regard to industrial action there is a requirement for votes at branches by show of hands or secret ballot. For action to be taken there must be a three-to-two majority of all those voting in favour of the action.

CPSA

The Civil and Public Services' Association: the president, two vice-presidents and 26 elected members of the national executive committee have been elected by an individual ballot of members since 1980. Similar procedures were also introduced for the election of section executives and officers as well as some regional officers. In 1981 these provisions were extended to include the election for a five-year period of the four senior full-time officers of the union. The current procedure is as follows:

> ballot papers, along with election addresses, are distributed by branch and sub-branch secretaries to members;
> the votes cast are aggregated at each branch, sub-branch or workplace meeting and then aggregated at branch level;
> the votes are registered on branch ballot papers, signed by the branch secretary, chairperson and scrutineer and forwarded to the national returning officer who aggregates all the votes cast.

There is also provision for referendums on any question. This is at the discretion of the national executive committee or at the request of branches representing a majority of the membership. Surprisingly, perhaps, the form that the referendum should take is not specified in the union rule book. Apart from this, the practice has developed in successive pay campaigns for workplace or branch meetings to be organized and for standard resolutions to be put, a vote taken and then aggregated with the votes cast at other meetings. These votes are usually by show of hands.

NUM

The National Union of Mineworkers: the president and secretary are elected by a national ballot of members; in contrast the vice-president is elected by ballot of conference delegates. The arrangements for membership ballots are determined by the national executive committee. Currently the areas administer the election. Ballot papers are distributed by the area officials to branches which are normally based on a single pit, workshop or office. The papers are then collected by members, filled in, and deposited in a ballot box. Branch officials collect the boxes, bundle up the papers, and fill in a return of who voted and who did not. The papers are then conveyed to a central point in each area, collected by an area official and taken by hand to the electoral reform society to be counted. Usually the national executive committee appoints between two and four assessors to observe the count. It should also be noted that members of the national executive committee (representing members in constituent areas) and full-time area officials (and executives) are also elected under similar procedures. Significantly, there is provision for membership ballots on major policy issues, including industrial action. In the case of national industrial action it is necessary for 55 per cent of those voting to be in favour of the action before it can proceed. Such ballots are conducted in the same way as for elections.

TGWU

The Transport and General Workers' Union: a variety of ballot procedures is used. Shop stewards are elected by members in a workplace or at a branch meeting either by a show of hands or a ballot. The general secretary is elected by a ballot of all members (as are trade group committee delegates from each region). In contrast, the trustees of the union are elected at the biennial conference by a show of hands. On matters which in the opinion of the general executive council affect the interests of the union or a region or a trade group, then the general executive council may organize a ballot of relevant members using any or all the following procedures: voting at branch meetings; voting at works, garages, and so on; postal ballot. In each case the ballots are supervised by regional committees. Ballot boxes are located at the regional and sub-regional offices or 'other suitable places'. Eligible members are issued with ballot papers and their membership cards are marked. Once the ballot has closed, scrutineers (or their equivalent) appointed by the regional committee count the vote, declare the result and post a record to the regional secretary who in turn notifies the general secretary.

AUT
The Association of University Teachers: the executive committee is elected by a secret ballot of conference delegates who are not required to seek a mandate from their branches. In the case of the elected officers of the union a nominating panel is established, composed of the president, such vice-presidents who have held office as president, and four members chosen from the delegates at conference and elected by a secret ballot of conference delegates. As the title suggests this panel is empowered to nominate members for election as officers of the union; delegates at conference then vote for the candidates so nominated. Alternatively nominations may be proposed by branches in opposition to the names put forward by the nominating panel. Such nominations must be added to the ballot paper.

The delegate conference is empowered to call industrial action or, if between conferences, the executive committee has this authority. There is also provision in this union for a ballot of the whole membership. The executive committee is empowered to recommend such a ballot to the conference and to specify the wording of the question or questions to be put to the membership. If conference agrees the ballot is conducted as follows:

> batches of envelopes containing the ballot material are sent to branch secretaries;
> the branch secretaries organize a secret ballot of members;
> the branch secretaries return the completed forms by post to the general secretary; they are then counted in the presence of the union's auditors;
> the result is published as directed by the executive committee.

Significantly, this variation in procedure arises out of the different traditions and history of these unions. As will be seen these different procedures can have a major influence on union organization and action.

Elections In TUC Unions

It is against the background of these differences that the general patterns of union organization can be traced out. Overall the TUC unions display a wide variety of practice in electing their national executives and full-time officers (where elected) and in the constitutencies involved in elections. But, in general, all national executives are elected and the election of full-time officers is a well-established practice. This contrasts with the popular picture often presented by politicians and some union commentators.

With regard to the full-time officers of unions, it would appear that election is relatively common, as indicated in Table 1. Of the 30 major unions covered in the Table, 18 of the general secretaries are elected rather than appointed. By appointment is meant advertisement, selection and recommendation of employment by a national executive committee or sub-committee thereof. In most cases such recommendation must be ratified by conference decision; this is usually a formality. Key to the practice of appointment is the possibility of employing somebody who was not previously a member of the union. Such a possibility is highly unlikely in the case of elections. In the case of other full-time officers, it is more common for these to be appointed; even so only slightly less than half (12) of these unions elect some full-time officers in addition to their general secretary.

Table 1 Election/appointment of senior officers, 1980

Election/appointment	Union Officers		
	General secretary	President	Other full-time officials
Appointment by executive committee	12	10	18
Election: life	9	1	4
period	9	19*	8

* A number are elected from within an elected executive committee.

Source: Industrial Relations Review and Report, No. 282, October 1982.

With regard to presidents (or equivalent) the practice is slightly more complicated. In this instance most presidents are elected from and by their executive committees. But where this is so it is usual for presidents to be elected in the first place to the executive committee through some sort of ballot. Where this does not happen it is generally the practice for

presidents to be elected by a ballot of members or their representatives or delegates.

If all TUC unions are considered, then it would appear that the election of general secretaries is relatively common in practice, as shown in Table 2. Assuming for the moment that all those 'not available' are appointed, it still leaves more than a third (38 per cent) of the general secretaries of the TUC unions elected on the basis of some form of ballot, ranging from the whole membership to mandated conference delegates. Of the elected general secretaries, half (50 per cent) faced an election involving the whole membership; the remainder were elected through constituency ballots, which may include mandated conference delegates, non-mandated regional delegates and block branch ballots. Very few general secretaries were elected on the basis of secret postal ballots, only 12 per cent in all. Most of the elected general secretaries were elected for life, although there are signs that some unions may be beginning to consider introducing more regular elections (e.g. NUM, UCATT, UCW).

Table 2 Election/appointment of general secretaries, 1980 (%)

Appointed	Elected	Not applicable	Not available
26	38	1	35

1. Election refers to some form of ballot involving all members or annual conference delegates or combination thereof.
2. It is usual for appointments to be ratified by annual conference or delegate meeting.

Source: J. Eaton and C. Gill, *The Trade Union Directory*, 1981.

A research project by an Oxford-based team confirms this picture. A detailed study of 102 unions found that only eight unions elected their general secretaries by postal ballot and more generally, half the general secretaries were elected by the union membership, while less than a third were appointed. Overall, it was more likely for general secretaries of white-collar unions to be appointed (usually by the national executive committee or equivalent) rather than elected.

Thus, a considerable number of unions elect their general secretaries (and other full-time officers). Even where general secretaries are appointed these appointments tend to be ratified, more often than not, by a delegate conference. In the case of elections, a variety of procedures is used, although relatively few unions elected their general secretaries through a postal ballot. It should also be noted that periodic election is unusual; most full-time officers are elected for life.

In contrast, all TUC union executive committees tend to be elected, although there is considerable variation in the constituencies for these elections, as indicated in Table 3. From this it can be seen that the constituencies for the election of executives included the whole membership, branch, groupings of members on a geographical or section (trade) basis and conference. It was most common for executive committees to be elected from geographical (25 per cent) or conference (17 per cent) constituencies. Again very few executive committees (5 per cent) were elected on the basis of secret postal ballots.

Table 3 TUC union executive committees 1980: constituency accountability (%)

Membership Postal	Other	Branch	Area/ region	Section/ trade	Conference	Other	Not available
5	4	6	25	4	17	2	38

1. Section/trade constituencies often complement other constituencies.
2. Conference constituencies include annual general meetings of the whole membership: a feature of small unions.

Source: Eaton and Gill, *The Trade Union Directory*

The Oxford study already referred to provides further information about the election of national executives. Of the 102 unions surveyed, only 9 elected their executives by postal ballot. A further 7 unions used a qualified secret ballot procedure. In contrast, 13 unions elected their executives through a procedure based on branch meetings.

Other ballots

In addition to elections many unions use ballots for the commencement, continuation or conclusion of industrial action, in particular strikes. And many unions ballot on pay offers and related issues. The National Union of Seamen (NUS), for example, decides whether to accept or reject the annual wage settlement by a postal ballot of members. In contrast the NUM uses membership ballots (organized at the pit head) to consider pay offers as well as to gain authority for strike action. Variations in practice can occur even within unions, largely depending on the circumstances of a strike, and the ballot procedure used may range from a show of hands at a mass meeting to a delegate conference. This may be further complicated by the tactics for declaring strikes official or not: it may suit the union to tacitly support unofficial action.

In contrast, where unions do not have provisions for ballots for industrial action, it is common to decide industrial action at delegate conferences. This is in line with the constitutional position of conferences as the sovereign bodies for policy determination. For this reason it is quite common for union executives to recall a delegate conference to consider national industrial action, particularly in public sector unions; for instance CPSA, NUPE, NUR, SCPS. Occasionally it is the case that unions must reconvene a delegate conference if a ballot on a pay offer or strike action is to be considered. The conference is then in a position to give authority to conduct a ballot. This is the case with the Confederation of Health Service Employees (COHSE).

More generally, it would appear that provision for strike ballots is relatively common in trade unions. Of the 102 unions surveyed in the Oxford study, 65 had some form of provision for strike ballots, with 25 unions requiring a ballot of members before an official strike could be called. By contrast, in 37 unions the responsibility for calling national strikes rested with the national executive. Only 6 unions made provision for the use of postal ballots for the consideration of strike action, although a further 8 had provisions for the use of qualified postal ballot procedures.

Even where unions have no provision to ballot members over strike action or on major policies, it is usual for them to consult their membership. This may include meetings of local stewards or workplace representatives to authorize or advise on industrial action, as is the practice in the Association of Scientific, Technical and Managerial Staffs (ASTMS). Other unions attempt to organize local meetings (based on workplaces, branches or areas) so that members are able to indicate their views on the proposed action. At times this amounts to something like a referendum of members in attendance at such meetings, as was evident with the consultation meetings held by the civil and public service unions during the 1981 civil service pay campaign.

Thus ballots are an integral feature of union structures. They range from a show of hands at a members' meeting to secret postal ballots. The most common form for the election of national union officials would appear to be the secret ballot. In contrast, there appears to be more variation in the procedures for considering industrial action and policy determination, although many executive committees have considerable discretion to call strike ballots for national action. The implication of this variation in procedure is that unions are structured and organized in different ways so as to enable a degree of membership involvement and participation.

6. Representing Members

This chapter examines two levels of union organization, workplace representation and national representation. I show that workplace stewards are now an integral feature of non-manual and manual unions. This development has been accompanied by the extension of steward facilities and the incorporation of stewards in union hierarchies. While this has been a fairly uniform development the organization of unions nationally is much more varied.

In this chapter I examine some of this variation, focusing particularly on the relations evident between conferences, national executives and paid full-time officials.

Workplace organization

Constitutionally, the branch is the basic unit of most unions, although there is considerable variation in the responsibilities and membership coverage of branches. They may be large and cover more than one workplace or employer. Some are concerned principally with union policy, while others are important units of organization for negotiations and the conduct of industrial action. To an extent, these differences are reflected in membership participation and involvement.

Branch size and composition
A recent national survey (1980), sponsored principally by the Department of Employment (DE) in conjunction with the Social Science Research Council and the Policy Studies Institute, provides some data on branch size and composition. According to this survey, branches may range in size from 10 or 20 to several thousand, although branches in manual unions tend to be large in comparison with those of non-manual unions. Half the manual unions covered by the survey had branch sizes ranging from 200 to 2,000. Table 4 shows the branch sizes of the major unions. The branch size for non-manual unions ranged from 100 to 900 members, as shown in Table 5.

Table 4 Branch size of selected manual unions, 1980

No. of Members	AUEW(ES)	GMWU[1]	NUPE	TGWU	ALL
Average[2]	989	979	812	580	861
Median[3]	750	483	443	293	438

[1] Now GMBATU.
[2] Average: The sum of the cases divided by the number of the cases.
[3] Median: The point on a scale of measurement, above which are exactly half the cases and below which are the other half.

Source: W. W. Daniel and N. Millward, *Workplace Industrial Relations in Britain*, 1983, p. 83.

Table 5 Branch size of selected non-manual unions, 1980

No. of Members	ACTSS/TGWU[1]	APEX	ASTMS	NALGO	TASS	ALL
Average	244	273	716	1253	471	681
Median	88	116	657	494	521	320

[1] ACTSS = The Association of Clerical, Technical and Supervisory Staff, the white collar section of the TGWU.

Source: Daniel and Millward, *Workplace Industrial Relations in Britain*, p. 84.

To a large extent branch size moves in line with branch composition. Three types of branches are described in the DE study: workplace branches, single employer branches, and multi-employer branches. According to the survey the following patterns were evident:

workplace branches: at least one third of the branches for the TGWU, ACTSS, and APEX were workplace-based;
single-employer branches: National Union of Public Employees (NUPE) and National and Local Government Officers' Association (NALGO) branches were principally single-employer branches, reflecting employment patterns in the state sector;
multi-employer branches: almost all the AUEW(ES) branches and at least two-thirds of the Amalgamated Union of Engineering Workers – Technical, Administrative and Supervisory Section (TASS) branches were multi-employer.

To facilitate workplace representation and negotiation, unions have occasionally established subsidiary levels of organization. In the following unions these structures have been designated as follows:

ASTMS	group
NGA	chapel
NUJ	chapel
SCPS	sub-branch
SOGAT 82	chapel
TASS	office committee

In these unions this level of organization has become very important.

Shop stewards

It is in this context that unions have established workplace systems of representation. The DE study showed that shop stewards are very much a feature of contemporary unionism. The survey covered 2,000 establishments across the whole of the manufacturing and service sectors (public and private) and revealed that three-quarters of the establishments where manual unions were recognized had one or more stewards; additionally there were senior stewards or convenors at half the establishments. Non-manual unions were less likely to have such workplace representatives: approximately two-thirds of the establishments where non-manual unions were recognized had at least one steward.

It was most common for stewards to be elected by show of hands of members at a meeting, as shown in Table 6. For both manual and non-manual unions, the majority of stewards were elected by a show of hands; although it was more likely for manual stewards to be elected in this way than for non-manual stewards. It was more likely for non-manual stewards to be elected by postal ballot (about 10 per cent of the cases covered by the survey) than for manual stewards (about 3 per cent). In addition, it was common for stewards to stand for periodic election (about three-quarters of the senior and ordinary stewards and just over half of the sole manual stewards and two-thirds of the sole non-manual stewards). In view of the propensity for election by show of hands, and the widespread practice of periodic re-election, it is evident that a feature of contemporary unionism is workplace systems of representation based on meetings of members with established procedures for formal accountability and control.

The survey indicated a correlation between the method of appointing senior stewards and the number of stewards representing groups of workers. According to the survey, in situations where there were few (less than 20) stewards then union members tended to elect a senior steward to

Table 6 Methods of appointment of workplace representives, 1980 (%)

| | Union representatives | | | | | |
Method	Senior[1]	Manual Ordinary[2]	Sole[3]	Senior	Non manual Ordinary	Sole
Show of hands	67	71	71	57	60	49
Postal ballot	3	3	2	11	9	7
Non-postal ballot	23	21	13	23	25	22
Other	3	5	7	4	7	10
No election	1	*	5	2	*	7
No information	3	–	2	3	–	5
	100	100	100	100	100	100

[1] Senior = the senior workplace representative in establishments with more than one steward.
[2] Ordinary = non-senior workplace representatives in establishments with more than one steward.
[3] Sole = only steward in the establishment.

* less than 0.5%

– zero

Source: Daniel and Millward, *Workplace Industrial Relations in Britain*, p. 87.

represent their interests. Conversely, if there were many stewards (more than 20) then it was more common for the stewards themselves to elect the senior steward. In part this probably reflected the practical exigencies of one procedure over the other rather than a preference on the basis of principles.

On the evidence of this survey, joint shop steward committees are not widespread. The report noted that only in a minority of multi-union establishments were joint shop steward committees set up; such committees were most likely in the larger establishments or those with several bargaining groups. They met relatively frequently: nearly half of the manual committees and just over a third of the non-manual committees met at least once a month with the majority of the remainder meeting at least once every three months. The vast majority of these committees (81 per cent of the manual committees and 76 per cent of the non-manual ones) conducted their meetings during working hours.

Meeting attendance

In view of these patterns of organization, membership attendance at meetings is obviously crucial, particularly if workplace representatives are to be accountable to and controlled by members. The evidence suggests that membership attendance at branch meetings is related to whether the branch is based on one workplace or more than one workplace, as indicated in Table 7.

Table 7 Membership Attendance at Manual Union Branch Meetings, 1980

	Workplace	Type of branch Single employer	Multi-employer	All
Branch membership	110	450	880	438
Attendance at meetings	23	35	32	30

Source: Daniel and Millward, *Workplace Industrial Relations in Britain*, p. 85.

Where a branch is based on one workplace, attendance is higher than for other branches. About one-fifth of the manual branch membership attended workplace branch meetings whereas attendance fell to about one-twentieth of the membership at non-workplace branch meetings. For non-manual unions the figures are one-third and one-twentieth respectively. This suggests that where there is provision and opportunity for workplace meetings membership participation is likely to be higher, a fairly commonsense supposition.

In some unions there is little or no provision for workplace-based branches. For example, the 1,217,760 members (in 1980) of the AUEW(ES) are organized into 2,600 branches, few of which are workplace-based. This gives rise to a number of problems which affect the way the union operates. With regard to membership organization and activity in the workplace steward-based structures have emerged and played an important part in the history of the union. Surprisingly, however, stewards have no formal contact with branches as they are subject to formal control by the district committees. Alongside this, workers employed on the same site may be members of any one of a number of different geographical branches. At a minimum this means that the collective consideration and development of union policy is likely to occur outside the workplace. In view of the more limited membership attendance at branch meetings outside the workplace the AUEW(ES) seems to be structured to ensure minimal membership involvement in the formulation and development of union policy.

Bureaucracy in the workplace?

Obviously the opportunity for workplace meetings is important but it is even more so when workplace representatives do not necessarily come into day-to-day contact with members. An indication of the degree of distance between such representatives and their members may be given by facility arrangements, which while improving the technical side of union work may well be bought at great cost to union vitality.

First, there has been a significant increase over the last eight years in the provision of office services for senior stewards, as indicated in Table 8.

Table 8 Facilities for Senior Stewards, 1980 (%)

Facilities	Senior stewards	
	Manual	Non-manual
Own office	20	18
Use of office	52	56
(Provided in previous 5 years)	(36)	(33)
Own telephone	23	30
Use of telephone	72	64
(Provided in previous 5 years)	(45)	(38)
Other office help[1]	73	84
(Provided in previous 5 years)	(33)	(31)

[1] 'Other office help' covers secretarial assistance, access to photocopier or access to a typewriter.

Source: Daniel and Millward, *Workplace Industrial Relations in Britain*, p. 43.

Many of these facilities were gained between 1975 and 1980, probably the result of the confident unionism of the time and the support given by the Labour government through legislation and policy. Alongside this in the larger establishments it was very common for full-time conveners to be recognized for manual workers (nearly two-thirds of establishments with 2,000 or more workers had full-time convenors for manual workers).

Second, check-off arrangements (deductions of union subscriptions at source by management to be paid over direct to the union) are widespread in the public sector as well as larger establishments in the private sector (e.g. check-off arrangements were recognized for three quarters of workplaces that recognized unions for manual workers). The importance of this arrangement is that the regular contact between stewards and members is no longer guaranteed.

These arrangements illustrate one of the major dilemmas facing the left when arguing and campaigning for more effective and democratic unions. Without doubt the campaigns in the 1970s for an extension of facilities, including training, were correct. They involved demands on management which if met helped to reshape the relationship between workers and their employers. Local representatives were in a position to promote the interests of members in ways that had not been possible previously. But these achievements had a sting in the tail in that local representatives enjoying the convenience of facility time and office support tended to become removed from the members they represented. These developments, in addition to the considerable expansion of consultative arrangements between managers and workers' representatives, have led some commentators to argue that the last ten years have witnessed the bureaucratization of unions in the workplace. So while gaining facilities in one period can be seen as a victory for workers' struggle, subsequently such achievement may inhibit the development of vibrant trade unionism.

But there is a further side to these developments which deserves mention, namely that senior stewards or convenors are often in a position to exercise considerable discretion in relation to workplace bargaining and other union activity. Apart from the possible gap between these stewards and their members, often they have little to do with paid full-time officials. The DE evidence showed that typically manual senior stewards contacted local full-time officers two or three times a year; non-manual senior stewards contacted their officers twice a year. Nonetheless, senior stewards at the larger establishments were most likely to contact local full-time officials. This contact concerned the main periodic pay negotiations as well as grievances and disputes. In addition, just under half the senior stewards had contacted a national official or head office in the previous year (although the actual incidence was not given). Again, it was most likely that senior stewards at the larger establishments made this contact.

Taken with the earlier evidence, it would appear that senior stewards are not tightly integrated with either their members or with paid full-time officials. This means that these workplace representatives are in positions to take initiatives on workplace bargaining, negotiations and other workplace union activity. While this does not mean that senior stewards necessarily act in this way, the possibility remains that they may do so.

National organization

As already indicated, there is considerable variation in the arrangements for union policy-making and the pursuit of union objectives. Formally, union structure is similar, based on the branch and ending with a conference (or equivalent) of members' representatives. However, underpinning this structure is considerable variation in the web of relationships that bind the union together. In this section some of this variation is examined.

Union structures

At the outset it should be reiterated that participation in unions depends upon many things apart from the formal structure. These include the following: the traditions of trade unionism; the character of the membership (staff or shop-floor workers, skilled or unskilled workers, men or women, black or white); the state of the labour market (buoyant or stagnant); the form of negotiating structures (remote or accessible, centralized or decentralized); and the political organizations and groupings active within the unions, including the left-inclined or right-wing leaderships evident in many cases. A fully elaborated account of union organization must be based on a consideration of all these factors and the way they come together to give rise to particular forms of union organizations and structures.

At the base of most union structures are the branches, but it often goes unnoticed that their form can vary from union to union. As already noted, branch size and coverage varies enormously, within one union as well as from one to another. Branches may range from a mere handful of members to several thousands. They may cover one workplace or a number of workplaces in a local area; some cover a large geographical area. In some cases the geographical cover of branches has reached the absurd proportions of extending throughout the whole country (e.g. the Society of Civil and Public Servants: SCPS).

Although branches are formally the locus for policy formulation and execution in most unions, it is relatively common for them to be based on some smaller unit of organization (e.g. the chapel in the print industry), or to coexist alongside another form of organization (e.g. the group in ASTMS). In the latter case, some unions are organized on the basis of a dual structure: a geographical branch is responsible for the development and implementation of union policy; the workplace group is responsible for workplace negotiations and representation. Occasionally this may involve a number of groups co-operating and co-ordinating their activity in order to deal with one employer. This type of organization is common in the ASTMS and the TGWU.

Beyond the branch, unions may be organized on the basis of a grouping of branches into districts (or equivalent). This may be done on a trade or section basis, or consist of a group of branches in a particular area. There may also be a regional structure, consisting of a grouping of districts or branches in a region. Obviously, there is considerable variation in the authority and autonomy of these different levels of organization, in part reflecting whether the union is centralized or relatively decentralized. This can range from the tightly controlled organization of the EETPU to the relatively decentralized federal structure of the NUM.

Union conferences
But it is at the level of national committees and organization that the significance of these different arrangements and procedures becomes most apparent. Here, the formal position in most unions is that a conference of some sort attended by delegates from branches, districts or regions formulates and decides the national policy. This is complemented by an executive committee. Even so, this is only the formal position; in practice considerable variation is evident.

Constitutionally, conferences are usually the sovereign bodies of most union structures. It is at conference that policy is proposed, debated and decided upon. But there is considerable variation in the composition, procedures and authority of conferences. As a result, it is not necessarily the case that conferences embody the wishes of members or even reflect their interests.

In other unions, conferences may be attended by delegates elected at area or district level or some other level of the union structure. Usually, the conduct of such conferences is similar to branch delegate conferences, although their scale is much smaller. The National Union of Railwaymen (NUR) for example (with 157,355 members in 1982 organized into 580 branches), holds an annual conference (annual general meeting) which in 1980 was attended by 77 delegates, one from each division (group of branches). In contrast, the Post Office Engineering Union (POEU, with 132,828 members in 1982 organized into 295 branches), holds an annual branch delegate conference attended in 1982 by 693 delegates. Obviously, these differences make for very different ways of conducting the affairs of the union.

In a few unions, for example the British Airline Pilots' Association (BALPA), there is provision for a meeting of all union members. But such provisions are rare, if for no other reason than size (BALPA had only 4,319 members in 1982). Even for the most committed advocates of mass meetings it defies imagination to have had a meeting of the 1,695,818 paid-up members of the TGWU in 1982 to debate and discuss union policy. For this reason alone, the delegate system would have developed.

More generally, delegates to conferences are usually instructed by the membership in some way, although this is a mandate of varying degrees. Conference delegates may vote in a particular way for a variety of reasons – as directed by a few members at branch meetings, their own political inclinations, what they imagine members may prefer, what they think may be good for the union, or as a result of debate or indeed lobbying by other delegates at conference. In themselves, none of these reasons may be undesirable, but none necessarily involves members in debate and discussion about the issues facing their unions.

Tensions?

Perhaps the feature most often commented upon is the relationship between conference and the executive committee. It is usual for executive committees to feel bound by conference decisions, at least at a general level. Although this may not mean the avid prosecution of a decision, and even occasionally it might mean ignoring decisions altogether, reasons are generally put forward as to why a decision could not be pursued. However, in a few unions, conferences are regarded as advisory only and not at all binding on executives. This is most clearly evident in the EETPU and to a lesser extent the AUEW(ES). The EETPU general secretary, Frank Chapple, viewed conference decisions as follows: 'Resolutions are resolutions and not the laws of the Medes and Persians.' Fortunately such sentiments are not publicly expressed by most other union leaders.

This tension between conference and the national executive may be a consequence of dual structures: one based on delegate arrangements and culminating in the conference; the other based on a quite separate ballot procedure to elect the executive committee. In these circumstances it is not uncommon to see a gap appearing between conference decisions and executive committee actions. This is evident in the AUEW(ES) and more recently the CPSA. In both unions, left-inclined conferences have made decisions which were not taken up with either enthusiasm or diligence by right-wing executives.

As a corollary to this development it should be noted that in most unions executive committees and national officials are placed in highly strategic positions in which they may appear to have a great deal of autonomy from the membership. This is partly a consequence of their experience in 'playing the game' and is partly due to the political resources available to them to maintain and consolidate a high profile in the union.

These personnel usually have been in the union for many years and are familiar with all the routines and procedures. Consequently they are in advantageous positions at conferences where policy is made; they tend to take leading roles at other levels of the union, in branches, district committees, and the like; they are involved in negotiations and are party to the agreements made; they speak on behalf of the union elsewhere. Under these circumstances the workplace member is a novice and at a disadvantage in influencing the direction of union policy and activity.

This familiarity with union procedures and activity is complemented by the resources available to executive committees and national officials to further the policies and activities they support. This was clearly illustrated by the IRSF case referred to above when the general secretary sent a letter supporting executive committee policy to every member of the union. Such an opportunity was not available to opponents of this policy. Similarly through union journals and newspapers senior union personnel, particularly general secretaries, are able to present policies in preferred ways. The current general secretary of the CPSA, Alistair Graham, uses his column in the union journal, *Red Tape*, to promote the policies he supports, often in a highly partisan tone. Alongside these resources, such leaders often have a degree of discretion over the use of union finances, whether to financially encourage and support activity and policy. Meetings may be timed to the best advantage of preferred policy options, for example by calling a special conference so late that some options could not be sensibly supported. Agendas can be constructed to create the most favourable circumstances for a particular viewpoint. Thus, union leaders have a variety of resources available to them to support and consolidate their positions of dominance in the union.

The effect of this is that executive committees and officials can play leadership roles in the union by proposing policy, persuading conference and engaging in debate and discussion with a less aware membership; this can easily give rise to manipulation and attempts to control and 'guide' a membership, often against its own judgement. Perhaps the latter feature of union organization has been most evident in the conduct and handling of strikes, particularly large-scale national strikes.

But the problem is more than the danger of manipulation and control of union memberships. It is the case that even non-manipulative leaderships have too much power over their members. By the positions they occupy, the experience they gain, and the limited forms of accountability in most unions, many leaderships are in positions to successfully pursue the policies they favour. Thus, the problem is the relation between leaders and members, not that some leaders are prone to manipulate the membership.

To illustrate, unions usually have arrangements for changing the rules by which they are organized and operate. This may be at a special rules revision conference or at a designated session at the union's periodic conference. On these occasions, the constituent bodies of the conference may propose changes to the rules. In practice major changes are usually proposed by the executive committee, often on the initiative of the general secretary. Through their dominance in the union and the informal influence they can bring to bear on conference arrangements and debate, they are often able to have their way on these matters. Of course, this is not always the case, as was evidenced by the 1983 POEU conference decision requiring the general secretary of a proposed union comprising the POEU and the CPSA British Telecom Group to be subject to periodic re-election. This decision was made against the advice of the executive committee (although the formal recommendation was to remit the proposal). Or, as already mentioned, the 1983 special IRSF conference rejected an executive committee proposal for secret membership ballots before strikes. On this occasion, the IRSF general secretary led the executive committee campaign for its proposals.

At the same time, it is as well to keep clearly in mind the distinction between an elected executive committee and full-time paid officials (elected or otherwise). In many unions there is a gap between executive committees, periodically elected and (however mediated) accountable to the membership, and paid, full-time officials, often appointed and, if not, usually elected for life. This often means that full-time officials effectively run unions. After all, paid full-time officials are responsible for the day-to-day affairs of the union; executive committees are only occasionally involved. Executive committees are often put in the position of attempting to control paid, full-time officials at the most general level. They require reports from full-time officials but this means they must rely on the particular interpretations advanced by these same officials. Often there is no way of knowing if officials are withholding advice or information that may be crucial to making a decision. In short, despite the representative position of executive committees and the formally subordinate position of many full-time officials, the relationship is often skewed to the advantage of the latter.

This account of union representation highlights some of the attendant problems, both at the workplace and at a national level. First, while the extension of workplace representation and facilities should be welcomed, it has recently been accompanied by processes which have led to a separation between workplace representatives and members. Second, there is evidence of considerable variation in the procedures and structures of national union organization, partly reflecting the different traditions and practices of employment. Nevertheless, common problems have emerged within unions, particularly with reference to the relations between conferences, executives and paid full-time officials. The problem for unions is who has power and under what circumstances.

7. Economics and Politics: The Fateful Separation

Economics and politics

Union democracy is about more than structure and organization. It is also about objectives. In Britain these have been defined mainly in 'economic' terms, with the result that unions have tended to define their concerns as 'non-political'; 'political' questions will be dealt with by a Labour government. It is these issues which I will be concerned with in this chapter.

The concern with trade union law

Unions have long been concerned with trade union legislation; in fact it could be argued that unions were born out of the struggles in the nineteenth century to repeal and change laws relating to combination, health and safety at work, and regulations on the conditions of work. More recently, unions have challenged the trade union legislation of both Labour and Tory governments. In the late 1960s, in response to the Labour government's policies to restrict trade union activity, unions acted to defend their most basic of interests, namely the right to organize and defend workers' concerns. On May Day 1969 for example, demonstrations were organized against the proposals contained in *In Place of Strife*. Subsequently unions protested at Tory legislation: 3 million strike days in protest at the Industrial Relations Act 1971, 1 million strike days against decisions taken by the National Industrial Relations Court. Under the Tories, this concern was broadened to include protests against wage policies: 1.6 million strike days against incomes policies.

Lately, however, trade union protests against anti-union legislation have been muted. For example there has been no general campaign against the Employment Act 1980 and 1982 and the Trade Union Bill 1983. This is explained in part by the deepening of the economic crisis which has sapped and undermined the confidence displayed in the early 1970s. Today, workers face job insecurity, unemployment and falling living standards. As retrenchment and restructuring has proceeded, unions generally have not been able to mobilize the membership against the current spate of legislation. And where the National Graphical Association (NGA) did, in the dispute with the Stockport Messenger at Warrington in 1983, the TUC refused to give support.

Unions and the Labour Party

Unions in general and the TUC in particular have looked to the Labour Party to resolve the problems faced through legislation, and to create a society where working-class people can prosper. In recent times this was most clearly evident in the 'social contract', from 1974 to 1979, when a public agreement was reached between the Labour government and the TUC, to the effect that the two wings of the labour movement would work together to build a better society in Britain. For the unions, this meant wage restraint and a degree of co-operation with industrial capital in return for social and industrial policies favoured by the unions. For the Labour government, this meant a *de facto* incomes policy, and policies of intervention in the economy as part of reorganizing and restructuring the industrial base of the economy. Obviously, these policies had an impact not only on what unions were able to do, but also how they were expected to behave.

The general point to make is that most union leaders looked to the Labour Party as their political partner. For many unions (altogether 50 in 1982), this has been associated with the affiliation of the trade union to the Labour Party; this includes such unions as the TGWU, GMBATU, AUEW(ES), NUM, ASTMS and APEX. This has given these unions an important role in selecting Labour leaders as well as determining Labour Party policy. Unfortunately, this influence has often been the result of the use of the block vote which has enabled union leaders to cast the vote of their total affiliated membership in conference debates and for the election of Labour leaders. This has meant that a relatively small number of individuals have often wielded considerable influence on the Labour Party. A second way in which affiliated unions exercise influence on the party is through the distribution of the union political funds. Under current legislation these funds must be expended on political purposes. If the Labour Party were not to receive them as direct affiliation payments, then it would be placed in a position of having to negotiate with unions for election contributions and other financial support.

One further way that affiliated unions have played a part is through the organization of the Labour Party conference. Ken Coates and Tony Topham, in *Trade Unions in Britain*, point to the fact that throughout the

1970s, five unions (AUEW(ES), GMWU, NUM, NUR, TGWU) occupied all five seats of the all-important conference arrangements committee, which among other things decides the conference agenda. In fact it has been claimed that this committee has deliberately distorted debates through the exclusion of particular types of motions; in the words of Coates and Topham: 'Conference management may be a fine art as well as a key to democratic development and sometimes the artistry may have exceeded democracy by a not inconsiderable factor' (p. 321). The point is that unions have been in a key position to influence Labour Party policy.

At the same time, non-affiliated unions have frequently looked to Labour governments for policies favourable to unions. Such unions include NALGO, CPSA, SCPS and the AUT. Although many of the policies advanced by the Labour Party are supported by official union policies, and many of the activists of these unions are members of the Labour Party, there has been a reluctance to affiliate, usually because the membership adopts the view that unions should be non-party political and because it is acknowledged that large numbers of members may support the Tory party, and more recently the Alliance parties.

Tory control

The established procedure for using union funds for political purposes (narrowly defined) was laid down in the Trade Union Act 1913, which required that union funds be used for a specified political purpose, such as support for the Labour Party, when approval had been obtained in a membership ballot. If a majority of the membership are in favour of establishing a fund, those who do not may contract out of the payment; to do this, they must formally notify their union that they do not wish to make such a payment. Altogether, of the 63 unions with a total membership in 1983 of 8.7 million, 7.2 million contributed to the political funds.

Recently the Tory government has questioned these established procedures. In this respect, the Green Paper *Democracy in Trade Unions* covered a number of issues.

First it argued that the establishment of such funds through a once-and-for-all procedure was unsatisfactory since many trade unions had set up their political funds shortly after the Trade Union Act 1913 was passed. In addition to these arrangements it was suggested that periodic ballots be held to affirm continuance of the political funds.

Second, it was claimed that the contracting-out requirement was not working 'satisfactorily in practice'. More specifically it was argued that some trade union procedures made it easier or more difficult for members to contract out. The conclusion drawn was that a more appropriate arrangement would be for members to contract in rather than contract out.

Third, it was argued that membership of the political party officially supported by the union should not be a condition for election to a senior union position or for holding office, as it is in some unions today (e.g. the NUR requires its main office-holders to be the union's delegates to the Labour Party).

Fourth, the definition of political objects was regarded as out of date and in need of broadening to include contributions to European members of parliament, contributions for radio, television, films and video, and printing and preparation of literature.

Fifth, it was claimed that the definition of 'political' as party political was too narrow, and should be broadened to include such 'political' organizations as the Labour Research Department or the Fabian Society. Under the 1913 legislation, contributions to these organizations could be made from a union's general funds.

Finally, the Green Paper questioned whether the collection of political funds should continue to be made through the check-off system, as is the case with most unions today.

In the event, if the Trade Union Bill is unamended, it henceforth will be necessary for unions to ballot members every ten years on the continuance of political funds. Restrictions will be placed on the use of those funds, especially if there is no ballot in support of them. And, the range of activities designated as 'political' will be broadened. On top of this the Secretary of State has said that clauses will be added on the question of contracting out if unions are unable to guarantee that they will voluntarily tighten up current arrangements.

The implication of this is that it will make it much more difficult for unions to pursue their political objectives as they see fit. Areas of discretion which have long existed will be removed by the new Trade Union Act. In addition these proposals constitute a threat to the Labour Party, which is already in a parlous financial state. To this extent the Tories are attempting to regulate the historical relationship between many unions and the Labour Party.

Unfortunately, union responses to these initiatives have been muted. The TUC, when faced with the Green Paper, made a tepid defence of the rights of unions to be political. In the words of the pamphlet, *Hands Up For Union Democracy*:

> Trade unions like other national organizations – employers, churches, charities – will always be in the business of trying to

influence the actions and the policies of the government of the day on a wide range of economic, industrial and social issues. They must do to protect their members' interests. And when the government goes down a road which we are convinced will create great economic and social difficulties, the trade union movement is entitled to put pressure on the Government to change course. All free union movements in the world do this (p. 35).

Further, the TUC notes that nearly half the TUC unions are affiliated to the Labour Party. (At the end of 1982, 50 unions were affiliated to the Labour Party and in 1983 the four largest unions contributed nearly half its income.)

What is missing in this response is any attempt at a strong defence of why unions should have political funds and why they should be able to use them as they see fit. Instead the TUC complains about the unfairness of the Tories and protests that business organizations are exempt from these restrictions. In fact the TUC does not even make the case that the legislation is specifically aimed at the link between the unions and the Labour Party.

At the time of writing, the latest development in this saga has been a proposal from the TUC general secretary, Lionel Murray (January 1984), that unions drastically rethink their current position and practice. Specifically, he proposed that unions should look at their internal arrangements, consider new ways to involve members and encourage workplace branches. To this extent Murray acknowledged that many workers, particularly the young, do not readily identify with unions or play a part in them. He also proposed that unions should voluntarily deal and indeed co-operate with governments other than Labour. In part, this is a retreat to the policies embraced by the TUC during the Second World War and on into the 1950s. To this extent the TUC has conceded the Tory arguments.

The rediscovery of politics

In general, union concerns tend to be narrow, primarily concerned with pay and conditions of employment. This concern obviously has its roots in the fact that unions in a capitalist society are the organizational form to express the collective interests of union members as workers, employed or otherwise. At the heart of this lies the employment relation as signified by pay and conditions of work. Without this concern unions would neither have a base nor be important to the working class. But while the employment relation has always been at the heart of their interests, there has been a broadening of concerns in recent years. After a period of quiescence in the 1950s and early 1960s, unions once again have found themselves having to confront governments if they wish to protect their central interests.

The background to these developments has included the recent rediscovery of political strikes. In part this was in response to the Labour government of the 1960s, sometime partner of national union leaderships, when policies to restrict union activity were proposed. The unions, in this situation, acted to defend their collective interests on the most basic of issues, namely the right to organize and defend the concerns and interests of workers. This history has been reviewed extensively in Chapter 2 but union action included: demonstrations on May Day 1969 against the proposals contained in *In Place Of Strife*; a strike in March 1970 by 22,000 dockers against the conditions under which the Labour government proposed to nationalize the ports; 3 million strike days in protest at the Tory Industrial Relations Act 1971; 1 million strike days against decisions of the National Industrial Relations Court and 1.6 million strike days against incomes policies.

Although the signs are few, unions have begun to broaden their concerns, albeit often reluctantly and tentatively. Perhaps the clearest, and most commented upon, development in this respect was the constellation of activity against public expenditure proposals and cuts in the mid 1970s. This included a range of activities, such as the campaigning of local union and community groups against closures and cut-backs, national demonstrations, co-ordination at a national level between some of the big state-sector unions and campaigning through research and propaganda. Though in terms of stopping cuts the results were limited, these developments did represent an attempt to extend the definition of unions, both in terms of organization and action as well as policies.

While this has been an important development, recent union responses to anti-union legislation have been very limited. At the time of the Industrial Relations Act 1971 the unions, under the auspices of the TUC, were able to mount a relatively successful campaign against the legislation. This, however, has not been the case with the union campaign against the Employment Act 1980 and 1982 and the Trade Union Bill 1983. Although there is a recognition that this legislation is anti-union, there has been no vocal and general campaign against it. It has been left up to particular unions to challenge the limits of the law, such as the NGA in their dispute in Warrington at the end of 1983.

To appreciate the significance of this shift it is necessary to note that unions provide one of the few means whereby workers can protect themselves and advance the collective interests of the working class. It is through unions, though not exclusively, that policies (e.g. employment, housing, racism, poverty, sexism) can be defined as union problems, at least in part, and solutions sought through collective organization and action. This is not to suggest that this will automatically happen, or indeed that it is very widespread at present. It is to claim that union organization, based as it is on the employment relation, offers one of the very few opportunities in contemporary capitalist societies to bring collective action to bear on these problems.

The defensive concerns of unions are obvious. In general, they have defined their interests quite narrowly, mainly limited to issues which directly and immediately concern workers, such as pay and conditions of work, legislation aimed at restricting union behaviour or guaranteeing the rights of trade unionists. For many unions, this has meant looking to the Labour Party for support and solace. But, this narrow focus was challenged in the 1970s when public sector unions in particular recognized in their campaigns and disputes the inextricable link between 'economics' and 'politics'. Nevertheless, this has been a tentative, and to an important extent, partial recognition.

8. What Is Wrong with Unions?

There are problems with unions today which make the case for union democracy urgent. Too often they are divided and concerned with a narrow range of issues, dominated by national officials and reformist. These are not isolated features but an interconnected set of problems. These interconnections will become apparent as I examine the arguments around each of these issues.

Economism

In general, union concerns tend to be narrow, as commentators have often observed. They tend to concentrate specifically on levels of pay and conditions of employment. If the activity of most unions is examined then it is evident that there is a preoccupation with these issues. This is so despite the activity of political groups within unions critical of these trends. Indeed it could be said that many of these groups have tended to focus on questions associated with economic militancy rather than other matters.

The contrast is often drawn between these preoccupations and the possibility of pursuing control over jobs or the content of work. It has been argued that the latter concerns are either fundamental or of particular interest to sections of the membership and thus should be pursued. For these reasons, it is argued, unions should broaden their concerns. This would then be a significant contribution to socialist struggle.

The argument can be developed further than this, particularly in relation to state workers. In view of incomes policies and state policies toward employment and the consequent restructuring of the state, union concern with pay and conditions of employment is also a concern with state policy and practice. Following on from this, I would argue that it is no longer possible to separate out 'economics' and 'politics' and pretend there is no relation between them. A fight for jobs or wages or safety at work either directly or indirectly is a fight against state policies and the prevailing relation between labour and capital. To this extent, union concerns and preoccupations with economic issues are also a concern with 'politics' and the way in which society is structured in ways detrimental to labour.

These issues have been taken up recently in the publication *The Forward March of Labour Halted?* (1981) which can be taken as representative of the broad currents of thinking on these questions. Three approaches emerge. First, a claim is made that the preoccupation of unions with wage issues is a major limitation on union struggles. At worst, such a preoccupation results in one set of workers being set against others. More commonly economistic preoccupations positively inhibit the achievement of a broadly based solidarity between workers (Eric Hobsbawm and for different reasons Hilary Wainwright). Second, in contrast, the inhibiting features of economistic unionism have been exaggerated. Some unions in some industries have been able to extend their role and activity so as to recognize that union struggle can cover a broad range of issues including wage struggles (Pete Carter). Third, unions have been necessarily and correctly concerned with wage issues and struggles. In this view workplace trade unionism is seen to be at the core of the 'daily struggle for power' by the working class (Steve Jefferys).

In the light of the debate about economism it is important that this issue is examined carefully. An initial general point is that the oft-noted distinction between pay and work control is overdone. What many commentators fail to realize is that in most wage issues there is an implicit concern with job control and control of work. Thus, it is claimed, even in this respect it is necessary to go beyond the superficial view that wages equal 'economics'. It is necessary to delve behind appearance and see 'economic' struggles in a broader light.

The problem is that the inextricable link between 'economics' and 'politics' is not recognized and the ideological segregation of 'economics' from 'politics' that is so prevalent becomes self-confirming. Such segregation has come to be seen by many as 'natural' through the history of the labour movement. It appears to be the way that society itself is organized. It seems to be affirmed through the institutional division in the labour movement between the Labour Party and the trade unions. The more that this separation is seen to be 'natural' then the more 'real' it becomes.

This, however, is not to deny that unions do have preoccupations with pay, jobs, hours of work, management authority and autonomy, health and safety at work, technological change and innovation, sexism and discrimination. Unions are concerned pre-eminently with the broad range of relations that fall under the headings of work and employment. But it must be remembered that these concerns are the product of history and struggle. They are not inherent to the union form of organization and action. Unions have changed their concerns over time, sometimes broadening their activities to include, for example, the concerns of the welfare state, sometimes narrowing their activities to fight a rearguard action to preserve some jobs, usually male, from dilution or technological extinction.

To this extent the charge of economism is misplaced. Unions need to be examined in their context and history. There is a material base to the way in which they have developed. Unions did not emerge out of thin air; they are rooted in the world of work and employment. And, at the same time, there is a material base to the way in which unions could develop. From their current position they have the potential to develop and mature in a variety of ways. This of course, is the hope for the future, and the reason why socialists should be concerned with the way unions organize and operate.

One of the reasons why union democracy is a pressing issue is precisely so that unions are able to fulfil their promise and in defending workers' interests advance the socialist struggle. It is through union democracy that members will be able to exercise their choice about the type of unions they want and the way such unions should develop. Only through union democracy will members be in a position to reject the fateful segregation between 'economics' and 'politics'. Only through membership participation and involvement will the narrow focus, and often sectional preoccupations with some issues, be overcome. It is in this way that militant economism can take its proper place as an essential ingredient of socialist struggle, as a crucial but not sole concern of trade unions.

Sectionalism

The issue of economism is often linked to a second set of problems, namely the divisions and separations between workers and the way these are often reflected in union organization and operation. This is the problem of sectionalism. It is the problem of divided and parochial unionism rather than solidaristic and united unionism.

Sectionalism refers to the divisions within unions as well as divisions which cut across those in and out of paid work. In this latter respect, there is a major division between those who are in paid employment and those who are not. Apart from differences such as work routines, income, dependence on the state or breadwinner, those without paid employment do not have access to broadly based, well-established political organizations like trade unions to express their concerns and interests. This means that those outside paid employment are also outside the major working-class organizations. The result is a fractured working-class movement.

Gender divisions are even more pervasive. They cut across paid and unpaid labour so that at all points women are more greatly disadvantaged and discriminated against. Women on average earn less than their male counterparts at every level of the employment structure. At the same time, women bear the burden of unemployment more directly and insidiously than men. The issue is compounded by the lack of concern and failure of trade unions to address these questions directly and actively, with the consequence that such divisions are reinforced rather than overcome.

Another set of divisions which cuts across waged and non-waged workers is that of racism. In view of the profoundly racist character of British society black workers are disadvantaged and discriminated against at work, in housing, in health services and provisions, politically, and, of course, in unions. Among the young, black youth are most likely to be unemployed and have very few prospects of paid employment. To an important extent, these divisions are reflected in union organization and action, although many unions have turned their attention to these matters, through policies and reorganization (e.g. recently NALGO). Thus the working class is further divided against itself.

Within the world of paid work, workers are divided by the jobs they do. In a single workplace, a school for example, there are many different jobs. At the most general level there is the teaching and non-teaching staff. But within each group there are further divisions – maintenance workers, cleaners, teachers, the head teacher, and so on. Different people have different concerns and interests depending on their jobs. To an important extent, these differences are reflected in the organization both between and within unions.

Jobs are grouped into management structures, which together distinguish one set of jobs from another. More precisely while the employer in a school is the local authority, in practice the school is managed by a head teacher acting within guidelines set by the education department of the local authority. At the same time, ancillary workers and teachers are supervised by head teachers but each may be answerable to different sections in the education department. Further, general education policy and practice is the responsibility of the Department of Education and Science. In this way complicated structures of organization and control further divide one set of workers from another.

Historically, one equally important way in which workers have been sectionalized is in terms of place of work. At the most basic level, workers are employed (or not employed) in different towns and cities, regions and countries. Within a locality members work in different offices, factories and other work sites. It has often been noted that this may give rise to a fairly debilitating parochialism. This has meant that workers have regarded themselves as belonging to a particular area, where the concerns of others elsewhere was neither seen as immediate nor as particularly relevant. While there are exceptions to this, it must also be said that despite trends toward more common working-class experiences, these views are still evident.

There are also important ideological divisions between workers. There are the employed and unemployed, which in the eyes of the state are regarded as 'workers' and 'scroungers'. Divisions between men and women are reinforced by notions of 'men's work' and 'women's work', 'proper' jobs and 'pin-money' jobs. Distinctions have been made between productive work (that is, work that makes a contribution to the economy) and 'unproductive' work (that is, work that depends on others for example, the 'pen-pushers' and the 'bureaucrats'). In these various ways divisions tend to be reinforced at the level of popular nomenclature.

All the same it must be noted that these are not irrevocable divisions. If they were then there would be no unions. In fact, it is to meet many of these difficulties that unions have organized. Unions enable workers doing the same or similar jobs as well as different jobs to recognize that they have common concerns and interests. Significantly such views can be extended to include those who do not work and who depend on others in paid employment. Unions provide one of the few opportunities for this recognition to develop. This may not be easy and certainly may occur at only a general level. Nevertheless, union organization is one way whereby this may develop.

Similarly, unions have organized so that common employment and other grievances can be acted on. They provide a base for unity about employer decisions and action. This is reflected in a union like NALGO, organizing staff employed in local government. In this union the occupational hierarchy is often reflected in branch organization. It has been common for senior local government officers to hold branch office. Recently this practice has been questioned through union nomination and election. In this way NALGO is beginning to move beyond management hierarchies and thereby establish the basis for unity and solidarity among local government workers.

The parochialism of the past is beginning to break down and is certainly a concern in many unions. Through meetings, conferences and joint committees, unions have challenged the basis of sectionalism. Obviously this is not easy and despite achievements that have been made divisive images abound about workers from different parts of the country, e.g. 'the militant Scot', 'the hard Yorkshire miner', 'the weak civil servant' and so on.

One of the reasons why sectionalism has not disappeared is because the residual strength of unions is to a certain degree rooted in sectionalism. Union members, understandably, have been and are concerned with immediate problems and issues relating to pay, conditions of work, job reorganization, the introduction of new technology and so on. For many members, union activity begins with the workplace; unfortunately all too often it has been difficult to extend union concerns beyond these immediate issues.

The dilemma for unions is how to draw on the strengths of sectionalism while at the same time going beyond it. Organizationally, the problem is which constituency should decide what should be done. In the event of a strike involving a section of a workforce should the workers involved make the decision to strike or should all the union members in the workplace decide? Or, should the semi-skilled TGWU members at BL be involved in a decision to take action that concerns toolroom workers? Or, who is to decide whether an issue is the concern of a section or trade group or all members irrespective of section or trade group (e.g. a common question in the two largest civil service unions, the CPSA and the SCPS)? These uncertainties have their roots in the dilemma of sectionalism and how to overcome it. In chapter 10 I shall spell out some of the principles of organization which I believe draw on the strengths of sectionalism while at the same time enabling it to be overcome.

Male chauvinism

There is considerable controversy about women in unions, although it is more or less recognized that women members are systematically excluded from the major activities and offices. Few women as a proportion of total women members attend the major events on a union calendar: conferences, branch meetings and so on. Similarly, few women hold office in unions: for example only one general secretary of TUC unions is a woman. While unions have been relatively happy to commit themselves to progressive policy objectives regarding the position of women at work, few have been able – some would argue, willing – to translate these into achievements.

Traditionally unions have looked to legislation to improve the conditions of women's employment and to remove forms of inequality and discrimination. But this has not resulted in either the elimination of inequality and discrimination or dealt with the general process of subordination at work or elsewhere. In these circumstances unions have begun to look at their own organizations as a necessary prerequisite for the achievement of these goals. This has often been in response to the arguments of women members that women are not able to be fully involved, in part because their specific interests have not been met.

Already a number of unions have introduced special arrangements to meet the needs of women members. These include:

special committees concerned with equality (ACTT, ASTMS, TASS, BIFU, COHSE, NALGO, NATFHE, NUJ, NUPE, NUT, SCPS);

reserved seats, particularly at a national level to guarantee the involvement of women at this level (TASS, COHSE, NUPE, TWU, TSSA);

special conferences for women members to debate policy concerning women (AUEW(ES), COHSE, GMBATU, SCPS, TGWU);

working parties on equality (APEX, BIFU, NALGO, NUT, SCPS);

appointment of persons with responsibility for women members (TASS, BIFU, COHSE, GMBATU, NUT, TGWU,); training full-time officers on legislation, negotiating guidelines and equality issues (ASTMS, TASS, EETPU, GMBATU, NUPE);

special education programmes for women members (APEX, TASS, BIFU, COHSE, GMBATU, NUPE, SCPS, TGWU, USDAW);

creche facilities for meetings, courses, conferences (ASTMS, TASS, COHSE, NATFHE, NUPE, SCPS);

publicity and information (ACTT, APEX, TASS, COHSE, GMBATU, NUS, SCPS, TGWU, USDAW).

Particular mention should be made of the NUPE reorganization in 1975. One of the purposes of this was to establish shop steward structures to enable the greater participation of women members. To an important extent this was successful, as signified by the increase of women stewards following the initial period of reorganization.

Although there has been considerable debate about women as union members, the most important point is that the vitality and future of unions depends on the involvement of women. This line of argument is clearly advanced by Jenny Beale in her book *Getting It Together*. She argues that internal divisions weaken unions by encouraging sectionalism. This is especially so where unions do not question or challenge the basis for gender divisions or reinforce these divisions through sexist attitudes and the way they are organized and operated.

Beale argues that women are a force for union democracy in at least three ways. First, they can challenge the prevailing structure and organization of unions in terms of differentiation and sectional priorities. In this way they may help to overcome some of the divisions that set worker against worker. In addition, measures for positive action (e.g. women's advisory committees and reserved seats on executive committees) can play an important part in enabling women to become more involved in unions.

A second challenge derives from the specific experiences of the women's movement. At their best the key features of organization developed in the women's movement have been characterized by their non-hierarchical and non-bureaucratic forms and their emphasis on widespread participation. Significantly the women's movement has shown the value of consciousness-raising activity, of allowing women time to develop their politics, for ideas to be shaped and developed through discussion, debate and supportive activity. This is in sharp contrast to the practice in most unions, with their formal hierarchies, procedures, remoteness and so forth.

In addition, Beale argues, women can bring to unions a rich political history which will enrich and contribute to union development and progress. Beale cites the campaigns for the vote, equal pay, maternity leave, and against public expenditure cuts, as issues in which women have been in the forefront; she outlines the way advances have been made on the questions of abortion, images of women, and sexual harassment. In these various ways women have made and can make major contributions to the overall union tradition.

However, some approaches to women and unions can be very dangerous and constitute an undermining of union democracy. In developing a critique against the representative political structure of most unions, some feminists have slid into the argument that every person should be their own representative. Such a view has been built on the experience many women have had in consciousness-raising groups and in women's centres, where the emphasis has been on participation and solidarity. Clearly, in this context this is an emancipatory and liberating activity and experience which should be sought and valued. However, it could be politically dangerous to transfer this to the operation and organization of unions; the view that each person is their own representative and indeed own person is in a union context profoundly individualistic; here emancipation and liberation have to be profoundly collective if they are to exist at all.

Jenny Beale is aware of these pitfalls and indeed advances the view that union democracy is about collective organization and action. The strength of the women's movement, for her, has been to translate these principles into practice. Thus in important respects the women's movement signifies the crucial features of union democracy; participation, involvement, commitment, collective organization and struggle. To this extent the women's movement is a model for the way in which unions could change and develop. What remains to be done is to elaborate on the way in which the experience signified by consciousness-raising groups can enrich and enable the development of a form of union democracy based on collective organization and action. This entails the recognition that unions are one of the few institutions which enable workers to defend their interests and fight for a socialist society. But the only way this can be achieved is by organization in opposition to capital: this requires combating the individualism of the capital relation with the collective organization and action of labour.

Bureaucracy

Perhaps the most extensive debate about political relations within unions has been cast in terms of the process of bureaucratization. At its simplest, it has not been uncommon for left critics of contemporary unions to present the issue in terms of a dichotomy between bureaucracy (signified by a stratum of personnel: full-time officials, national leaders and so forth) and the rank-and-file (workplace members and their shop stewards). The argument is that the structure and organization of unions is such that the bureaucracy has dominated and indeed manipulated the rank-and-file. Only through strong and active workplace organization can this be resisted and unions steered in a progressive direction.

In the last decade this question has been explored most consistently by Richard Hyman. He has argued in 'The Politics of Workplace Trade Unionism' that there are very strong forces for bureaucracy in unions which make the achievement of democracy partial and tentative. More than this, Hyman argues that the notion of bureaucracy needs to be examined as a set of relations which 'permeate the practice of trade unionism' rather than a stratum of personnel opposed by the rank-and-file.

The process of bureaucratization in unions, Hyman argues, is the outcome of three influences. First, as a result of their position as guardians of the union, officials are likely to adopt a cautious and conservative approach to the policies and activities of the union. Second, because of the 'rules of the game' officials become enmeshed in stable and predictable sets of relations with employers and the state. Third, there is a 'natural' tendency for the officials to defend unions in a way which emphasises their own competence and expertise. Taken together, these forces are likely to mean that officials will act cautiously and with concern for continuity and stability rather than as leaders of mass activity and struggle.

Hyman then summarizes a popular left-wing view, which is that stewards are the spokespersons of a rank-and-file which by implication are major opponents of bureaucratization. It is at the workplace that union concerns and preoccupations are necessarily broadened beyond the cautious economistic concerns of officials, where good shop stewards' committees have helped to counterbalance the tendencies toward workplace fragmentation and isolation and where the proximity of stewards to rank-and-file members means that bureaucracy and accommodation are less likely.

Against this view, Hyman shows the extent to which the last 15 years have seen the development, integration and bureaucratization of steward hierarchies as part of union structures. For Hyman, this signifies the 'bureaucratization of the rank-and-file'. The result, he claims, is that steward leaders now play a major role in containing and curbing union members.

Hyman makes two qualifications to his own argument. First there are enormous variations in the traditions, institutions and contexts of British trade unionism. This means that while there may be a tendency toward the bureaucratization of the rank-and-file, which for Hyman takes the form of a centralization of union activity, this is far from general and uniform. Second, the tendency toward centralization is not wholly undesirable since it signifies the process of overcoming the traditional fragmentation of workplace struggles. It is necessary, Hyman argues, 'for both leadership and discipline within shopfloor organization'. Only then will it be possible for the depredations of capitalism to be opposed.

Hyman's argument is not that bureaucracy is inevitable; on the contrary, he argues that the pervasiveness of bureaucratic relations, particularly in the workplace, is the product of recent union history. It has developed in the context of the increasing concentration of capital and the 'professionalization' of bargaining arrangements over the last two decades. In Hyman's view, unions did not necessarily have to respond to these developments through the consolidation and extension of bureaucratic relations throughout their hierarchies. There were alternative ways of responding to these changes, such as fighting for the extension of union democracy. The problem is that a number of unions with long traditions of workplace organization and activism did not choose this option (e.g. the TGWU and the AUEW(ES)).

The theoretical underpinning of this argument is that there is a radical dualism in trade union practice – between autonomy, on the one hand, and incorporation on the other. Thus according to Hyman, the history of recent trade unionism has been a history of the shifting balance between autonomy and containment so that steward organization can no longer be viewed as the vehicle of union opposition and resistance to capital.

His conclusion is therefore pessimistic: union democracy is only partially and tentatively attainable. But union democracy is nonetheless worth struggling for in the sense that unions are the basis for collective struggle both against as well as within capitalism, as an agency which can only ultimately be effective as a means for the collective mobilization of the working class. Hyman, however, observes that such a view has at best been marginal to the dominant traditions of unionism in Great Britain.

There is however, another way of looking at this question. If the broad contours of Hyman's analysis are accepted, and it is quite persuasive, the analysis, nonetheless, can be extended as a defence and indeed argument for union democracy. For Hyman goes beyond many of the less adequate left analyses of union bureaucracy, where the focus is on the role of a stratum of personnel who dominate, manipulate and restrain. Instead he makes the telling point that the issue of bureaucracy concerns sets of relationships which under certain circumstances may permeate the 'whole practice of trade unionism'. But if this is the case we can see union democracy in exactly the same terms. That is, union democracy is not about a stratum of rank-and-file personnel, union militants, who fight for more democratic structures and ways of operating. On the contrary, union democracy is about relations which should permeate the whole practice of trade unionism. Bureaucratic relationships need not be inevitable as Hyman suggests: democratic relations should and can inform and define trade unionism.

At the same time it is important to counter the impression that bureaucratic relations are an inevitable feature of contemporary capitalist society. When such an impression develops, bureaucracy can come to be seen as a way of organizing which is 'natural' and an evolutionary outcome of the changes in capitalist society. The more that such developments are regarded as 'natural' the more 'inevitable' they do in fact become. In view of this, it is even more important to campaign and fight for union democracy as an alternative and necessary way for unions to organize and operate.

Of course if this analysis is accepted, it means that union democracy must be fought and argued for. It will certainly not be achieved readily and easily, not least because of the context and traditions which are a mark of most unions. Nevertheless, if unions are to realize their potential as collective organizations engaged in struggle both within and against capital, it is essential that they are organized and structured in terms of democratic relations which permeate their whole practice.

Labourism

It can be argued that the ideology of unionism today is unremittingly reformist – characterized, that is, by a belief in the necessity and desirability of accommodation and compromise achieved through the procedures of collective bargaining. As part of this view there is the almost wholesale acceptance of parliamentarianism as the principal means for achieving change and progress in the wider society. As has been noted, there is an assumption that unions are weaker than employers in their partnership in industry. While the unions defend the working class in their workplace it is the Labour Party, the political wing of the labour movement, which is presumed to defend the working class more generally and to lay the foundation for gradual progress and improvement. Together the partners mould a new future for the working class.

Such a view has been elaborated by Hugh Clegg, in particular in the successive editions of his classic work *The System Of Industrial Relations In Great Britain*, but also by many other writers. It is predicated on an acceptance of the present. That is, it is based on a view that the current arrangements of society are broadly satisfactory, although clearly subject to improvement. Often this acceptance is placed against the backdrop of hardship and poverty in the past. There has been improvement, and slowly a basically fair society has been moulded and shaped. The industrial and political wings of labour have worked well together in the past. The problem now is the particularly vicious face of the current government, not any basic flaws of capitalist society.

This then is an ideology in which class relations are reflected in individual and representative terms rather than in terms of collective organization and action. Thus the achievements of the last century, so it appears, were made in the context of parliamentary democracy and its associated practice of collective bargaining. It is claimed that the working class has been well represented and well led even when unsure of the path forward. The unions, on the one hand, and the Labour Party on the other, have provided the means for progress. And, it is argued, they will continue to do so, despite current contretemps, and perhaps by the articulation of a more radical parliamentary programme. In this view, insofar as anything has been achieved, it has been through representation and the involvement of the individual member of the working class, the voter, trade union member, Labour Party supporter.

The problem with this view is that the relation between labour and capital is presented in individualistic terms. At no point is there any recognition that progress might require collective organization and collective struggle. For that would necessitate a radical reassessment of the relationship between the Labour Party and the trade union movement and a much sharper view of the nature and purpose of trade unions themselves. Although there are signs of some reassessment it is in terms of giving the Labour Party a 'broader' appeal or of the trade unions reaching an accommodation with the SDP. There are no signs of any more radical assessment.

As already noted, parliamentary politics are essentially representative politics. They are predicated on a view of society as composed of aggregates of individuals who may be members of unions or political parties, work or not work, go to church or not, and so forth. Against this it is necessary to assert the primary importance of collective organization and struggle in advancing, and indeed defending, the interests of workers. This view, which focuses on struggle, conflict, antagonism and contradiction between labour and capital, requires a reassessment of unionism. Such a view sees union democracy as essentially being about collective organization and action, which is important in its own right but is also bound up with the struggle for a socialist society. This, of course, means that the struggle for union democracy is a struggle that goes beyond the conception of politics articulated by the Labour Party. As such, it is associated with a belief that ultimately the only way that workers' interests can be advanced is through a struggle that is both within and against capital. Thus, union democracy in this view is both a precondition for as well as the means toward the development of a socialist conception of politics.

So, union democracy is an urgent question for unions. If they are to represent and realize their members' interests, meet the challenges of particular governments, and deal with the problems of a rapidly changing society, then they must be in a position to define issues broadly. Too often, unions have not been able or willing to do this. Only through a commitment to the principles of union democracy is there any possibility for unions to realize their potential. It is to this that I now turn.

9. The Basis of Union Democracy

Before outlining the principles of union democracy I shall examine briefly the circumstances under which unions must organize. First I shall consider the necessary roots of variation in union structure and organization. This will be followed by a discussion of the class nature of unions. In this I shall follow up earlier threads in my argument.

The roots of variation

I have noted on a number of occasions that there is extensive variation in union structures and organization. In some unions this is the result of conscious decisions to organize in particular ways, although such decisions may have been accompanied by considerable debate and controversy (e.g. the recent histories of the AUEW(ES) and the CPSA). But, more generally, variation arises out of the circumstances of the employment relation, particularly employment concentration and management structures.

Employment concentration
The immediate basis for variation is employment concentration. This has often been considered a key factor in unionism, the argument being that there is a greater propensity for union activity when the union is based on large concentrations of members in few worksites. In these circumstances members work together, readily identify issues and grievances as collective and thus union problems, act together to deal with issues at meetings or together in industrial action, know their workplace stewards and give support to each other in their unionism. Thus the principles of collective organization and action are manifest in the employment situation of these workers.

In these circumstances, it is relatively simple for unions to organize so as to reflect these concentrations of membership. Perhaps the best example is the pit organization of the NUM. In view of the concentration of members at each pit it is relatively easy for the union to focus administration, negotiation and representation at this level.

More generally, there has been a long-term trend toward the rationalization and concentration of capital, in Britain as elsewhere. This has meant that workers are more and more likely to be employed as part of large workforces, in factories and offices. It also means that even where there are relatively few workers on site (e.g. at a school or a high technology research unit) they are often part of a larger workforce employed by a single company or a section of the state.

While in theory these developments should make it easier for workers to organize as members of unions, it has still been difficult in the case of workers who are physically isolated and separated from each other. This is a particular problem in local and national government employment, but it is also a common feature of employment in the service sector and the building industry. The problem is that in these situations the support and strength gained by working alongside others is absent. Instead, the isolated member or members, often in hostile conditions, must take the initiative in playing a part in the union, approaching unknown stewards or officials and tackling local employers without the support of others. In these circumstances unionism is hard work, and the alternative of remaining silent and suffering can seem a better fate.

The usual response by unions in these conditions has been to organize on the basis of a geographical structure. Thus, all the members in a geographical area are grouped together as members of one branch, irrespective of concentration, employer, function or grade. In this way isolated members are given the support and sustenance that comes from being a member of a body that covers more than one workplace or employer.

Management structures

An account of the significance of the workplace for union organization and activity would not be complete without considering the relations between workers and their management in the workplace. Obviously, supervision is a feature of worklife. In all but the most unusual employment situations (e.g. home-helps) workers are accountable to an immediate line supervisor. These supervisors may have a greater or lesser degree of authority over workers for whom they are responsible. Some have relatively limited personnel supervising functions; others have the right to hire and fire, negotiate on local conditions and even wage levels. Such features of management practice can have a bearing on the form and character of union organization at a workplace level.

In recent times, there has been a reasonably well-established tradition of local workplace negotiations in manufacturing industry. This pattern emerged against a background of national negotiation over wage settlements in the 1940s and 1950s, in particular the push for wartime production which spawned workplace-based management-steward consultative committees. Toward the end of the 1950s, particularly in the motor industry and associated industries, some unions (especially the TGWU) campaigned for local bargaining arrangements and developed workplace-based local union structures to further this objective. This was extremely successful and stewards in this industry developed political importance and prominence. Significantly, this challenge from the shopfloor meant that managerial structures changed so that workplace negotiations could take place.

In contrast many unions have had no workplace organization, at least until recently. This is particularly so in local government, health services and national government. At a general level union organization in these areas is a clear example of the way in which management can structure union membership. Although this does not mean that unions are prisoners of management structures, it may mean in practice that unions in some areas are severely constrained by employers and associated negotiating machinery. Unions can and indeed have been drawn into the management structures and so begin to replicate management.

To illustrate, those civil service unions which organize the main administrative grades reproduce the structures of management as embodied in the Whitley arrangements, namely the joint management-union committees that consider different aspects of employment. Specifically, unions are organized to coincide with successive levels of the Whitley structures, locally, regionally and nationally. In this instance unions tend not to be organized on the basis of workplace structures. Local management and the Whitley machinery tend to cover a number of workplaces. Often this means that workers in the workplace see the union organization as something above and beyond them. Such arrangements may be justified by the spread of many workers over numerous workplaces, but this is not the reason for their emergence.

The other danger may be that members only see the union as concerned with and part of workplace relations. This can happen in areas where there have been key sections of workplace organization and activity but where there are no immediate and relevant connections between workplace union organization and the wider union structure. To a certain extent such a separation is guaranteed by the type of organization typical of many ASTMS branches and their constituent groups.

The class basis of unions

The way that unions must organize is determined to an important degree by the two basic features of the employment relation, employment concentration and management structures. But underlying these features of employment are class relations. Specifically, union members are working class and the possibility of union organization and action arises from this circumstance.

In the most abstract terms, being working class means having to work for someone else, receiving a wage and being subjected to a set of coercive and exploitative relations. And it would seem that this determines the common class interests of the working class. But in practice it is more complicated than this. There are many other factors which may inhibit the recognition of class position and provide for alternative ways of looking at the world. These may include such factors as gender and race and being employed or unemployed, as well as the political traditions of working class organization and activity.

In the case of manual workers, with their long traditions of trade unionism, it seems clear that class provides the basis of this form of organization and activity. This does not mean that there are no difficulties or unevenness in union organization; it is to point to the likelihood that manual workers are able to recognize their common class interests, albeit on a narrow range of issues.

Nonetheless, one of the major difficulties that workers face is the way in which managerial strategies inhibit the recognition of common class interests. To illustrate, there is a general and debilitating distinction drawn between manual and non-manual work, with the result that trade unions are distinguished as being predominantly either blue- or white-collar. Unfortunately, the extent to which these differences are accepted as 'natural' and 'inevitable' further serves to reinforce the divisions between manual and non-manual work, thereby inhibiting the recognition of the common class position of both types of workers. Paradoxically it has also led to certain sections of the manual workforce seeking staff or non-manual status.

It is against this background that some writers on class have advanced different versions of a 'proletarianization' thesis, namely that non-manual work is increasingly becoming like that of manual workers. As part of this, it has been argued that the increasing rationalization and concentration of capital has contributed to these developments through the breakdown of employment structures which formerly served to reinforce the differences between manual and non-manual work. For instance, large concentrations of lower-grade civil servants working in the same office are in a very similar position to factory workers and the routine involved in lower-grade clerical work is much like factory work. Unionism in this instance is seen as a specific means to realize particular and limited goals.

The problem with the 'proletarianization' thesis is that class position is understood simplistically. More adequate theories rest on understanding class in the context of complex and contradictory relations between labour and capital. For instance, non-manual work can be seen as being made up of two kinds of functions. A supervisor's work, for example, usually involves tasks necessary for production (like arranging for the smooth flow of materials as and when required). At the same time, supervisors manage other people. Of course, non-manual work need not necessarily be part of the production process as such. Bank workers, for example, are not directly involved in production but their services, as with those of clerical workers, book-keepers, accountants and so on, are ones which are essential to the capitalist process. Nonetheless, these people are waged workers, as are factory workers, although they do not necessarily see themselves in this way.

With regard to state employment specifically, this means that two features must be considered in assessing the class position of state workers: the duality of job function and the part played by state work in the capitalist process of realizing profit. Significantly, recent events which have thrown state workers into prominence are a consequence of attempts to restructure the state as part of the process of re-establishing the conditions for profitability and the expansion of capital. Thus state workers are ambiguously located: they are both part of the state which is attacking workers' interests, and workers whose interests are being attacked.

It is against this kind of background that variations in the contours and character of unions become understandable. Obviously at the most general level, unions have been born out of the class traditions and experiences of workers in their offices, factories, schools and so forth. But despite variation there are broad patterns of discernible similarity. The most important and fundamental of these is union organization as a class expression of workers' positions as sellers of labour-power, whether manual or non-manual workers. When identifying the principles of democratic unionism this must be borne in mind.

Clearly unions differ depending on their membership. Manual workers are more likely to be favourably disposed toward collective organization and action, thereby recognizing their common class interests, albeit in a limited way. In contrast, non-manual workers do not necessarily find trade unionism as easy or as readily available as manual workers. Even so, for all workers to be in a position to defend their class interests, particularly at the workplace, unions must be organized and structured according to the principles of union democracy. It is to this that I now turn.

10. Unions in the Workplace

For most union members, active involvement in the union begins and ends at their place of work. They pay their subscriptions, usually by direct deduction these days, receive reports from local stewards, or in the case of some unions a branch officer, occasionally receive circulars and journals, attend meetings of their section, occasionally attend mass meetings and occasionally attend branch meetings. It is in these ways that unions come alive for many members.

In this chapter I develop the argument that branch organization must be workplace-based and branch representation structured around workplace stewards. Only when unions are rooted in the workplace will members be able to play a full part in union organization and activity.

The branch

In many unions, the branch is the basic unit of organization, administration and representation. Formally speaking, it is through branches that members participate and become involved in union activity, particularly with respect to policy formulation and determination. For this reason, branches periodically organize membership meetings to consider branch business. More frequently a branch executive will meet to consider the day-to-day affairs of the branch, to draw up plans and proposals, organize action, make representation within unions, and occasionally participate in negotiations.

There are however, many variations to branch organization. In some unions the principal basis is the employment structure (e.g. the CPSA and SCPS). In others the principal basis is geographical location, such as the town (e.g. the AUEW or ASTMS). In some unions, branches are based both on the workplace and employment function (e.g. the ISTC where all members on one site are organized into one branch, or at large integrated works where separate branches cover departments or processes or type of work). In the EETPU there has been an orchestrated trend from the workplace to the specialized or industrial branch based on the amalgamation of branches covering a specialty or industry.

One common feature of many unions, which arises out of the demands of negotiation in the workplace, is that where a branch covers more than one workplace or function or employer, subsidiary levels of organization have been established (e.g. the group). Many unions depart from the principle of workplace-based branches. The reason for this may range from the attempt to consolidate and ensure central control in the EETPU to that of size and the dispersion of members in small numbers over many workplaces.

Members may be distinguished from each other by employer, function, grade or geography. Such divisions can be aggravated by a branch organization which manifests these divisions. There are a number of ways this can occur. In some unions, branches are organized on the basis of the employer, employment structure, function or grade. For example, branches in the CPSA and SCPS are organized by civil service departments. This effectively means that members from different departments are separated from each other even where civil service workers are based in the same or in nearby buildings. In like manner, it is not uncommon for ASTMS groups to be sectioned according to grade of worker. Clearly where this happens the grounds are laid for exacerbating the divisions and differences between workers in the same building or workplace.

In contrast some union branches are organized on the basis of geography, irrespective of employer, employment structure, function or grade. Since for most union members, active involvement in the union begins and ends at their place of work, geographical organization may be associated with the problem of non-involvement. This comes about because branch activity does not seem immediately relevant and meetings may not be held at convenient times and places.

At its worst, branch organization under these circumstances can manifest itself as sectional, parochial with a narrow disregard by members in one area or building or in one grade or function for the interests and opinions of those in other areas or buildings or grades or functions. This can mean that members prefer to keep to themselves, to keep others at arm's length or to worry about their own concerns.

So, it is possible that union organization itself gives rise to division between members, in terms of employment structures, function and grade. At the same time employment of different employees may also frustrate the construction of unity even though members are all in one branch. In both instances members may regard themselves as primarily concerned with the work of particular sections of the membership rather than with the membership as a whole.

The importance of these observations is to underline the necessity of considering the chances of membership participation and involvement in the operation of the union. At the most general level, this requires that unions be structured and organized in relation to the working lives of members and the employment relations in which they are enmeshed. On this basis, it would be possible to build a branch organization in which members' interests can be expressed, represented and met.

Workplace branches

The primary rationale of branch organization must be to enable and enhance membership participation and involvement. In this respect, branches should be the basic unit of organization in the union, with the responsibility for administration, delegation, negotiation and membership mobilization. To make this possible the following criteria should be met:
1 Since employment for the same employer provides the initial basis for unity, branches should be established wherever members employed by a single employer are located at one workplace in sufficient numbers.
2 Following on from this principle, where members are located in sufficient numbers in a locality (say, no larger than a trades council area), then that membership should also constitute a branch. In this situation each workplace should be represented on the branch executive committee.
3 Even so, in some unions this would still mean that some members remained outside the employer-based branch structure. Only at this point should unions consider geographical branches, irrespective of employer. Such members could be grouped together into amalgamated branches and efforts made to represent each workplace on the branch executive committee.

It may be argued that such branch organization would result in 'first class' and 'second class' branches, namely employer-based branches and multi-employer branches. More specifically, some branches would be able to relate directly to the employers whereas some would not. It could also be argued that amalgamated branches would have little to consider collectively since they would not be united by a common employer.

Against this, it needs to be asserted that where members are dispersed in their ones and twos across different employers the opportunities provided by employer-based branches are denied them. In these circumstances, a locally based multi-employer branch does at least offer some opportunity to play an active part in union life. Where this is complemented by a system of workplace stewards speaking to employers on behalf of members, and linked with other workplace stewards representing members working for the same employer, irrespective of branch, then the basis for involvement and participation is laid.

When these points are met, then the basis is laid for the union organization to be underpinned by the principle of participation. In this way, all activity is subject to democratic control and the effectiveness that comes from active and involved commitment is ensured. Only then will unions be able to meet the challenges from employer and state.

The steward

Stewards or representatives have become integral to most unions in the United Kingdom. Statistically, there has been an enormous expansion of workplace steward structures beyond the traditional industries (particularly engineering) in which such structures were initially established. This means that stewards are now a feature of trade union organization and involved commitment is ensured.

At the outset it should be noted that workplace steward structures vary considerably. Some stewards have responsibility for negotiations, representation and organization while others may be stewards in name only with such activity being the responsibility of others. To a large extent, this is a reflection of the traditions and forms of representation in different workplaces, industries, unions as well as the circumstances of class.

Clearly workplace stewards emerge in a variety of ways. The two most common would seem to be election by members in a workplace and appointment by branch (or equivalent) committees. This variation also reflects the different experiences and traditions in unions regarding the role and position of workplace stewards. Where stewards are appointed, the authority and accountability of executives for union life tends to be affirmed. In contrast, elected stewards are subject to membership recall and control. They are responsible to their membership in a more direct and immediate way.

The significance of these developments and practices is that organizationally the workplace steward signifies the first layer of democratic representation in any union. But this is a layer of representation and union activity which has undergone considerable change partly reflecting the changed strategies pursued by managements toward unions. In brief there has been a tendency to move from 'direct democracy' to 'representative democracy'.

The emergence of stewards

This change has been outlined by Michael Terry in an interesting recent study of 'shop steward development and managerial strategies'. He argues that workplace steward activity in the 1950s and 1960s was characterized by certain features which have now changed. First, workplace stewards were subject and party to an embryonic form of 'direct democracy' – meaning a close identification by the stewards with workplace members, membership control and accountability to the members. Second, workplace stewards were key members of a relatively autonomous and parallel level of organization in most unions. They were key figures in workplace activity. Third, this often involved negotiation between stewards and first level supervisors and the like. In this respect, this activity and organization did not have the formal approval of management; nevertheless there is evidence to suggest that management recognized these negotiations. Fourth, this activity was directed toward wage bargaining and was part of that process. This workplace activity was a particularly successful form of economic militancy, although it often extended to issues of job control. All the same this was a form of organization that developed only in particular industries. It signified an organizational response to a situation in which groups of workers had considerable local bargaining power.

The situation, Terry argues, changed with the deepening crises of British capitalism from the mid-1960s onward. First, restructuring of the private sector through mergers, takeovers and so on required new levels of union organization (e.g. combine committees) to meet these changes. Second, centralization of wage bargaining in the private sector placed negotiating demands on stewards who were often ill-equipped to deal with them. Third, managerial techniques of control were enhanced with the extension of work-study and job evaluation. This effectively formalized the links between work and pay, subjecting it to central control. Again, this placed pressure on stewards to organize beyond the immediate work group. Fourth, wage payment became less individual and more uniform and standard, subject to centralized bargaining. Fifth, management adopted a series of strategies which had the intention of integrating stewards into the formal industrial relations procedures – check-off, full-time steward status, facilities and so forth.

At the same time, pressures developed within the state sector where unions faced increased pressure for workplace- or at least local-bargaining. This was often accompanied by the need for unions to mobilize their membership, although they only had imperfect means to do this, having no tradition of steward organization. This meant that a number of unions reorganized so as to promote, or even sponsor, workplace steward structures. Where this occurred, as in NUPE, it was common for the stewards to be highly integrated into the prevailing union structures.

Thus there has been a pressure toward forms of representative democracy, with the focus on the way in which representatives are chosen rather than on members telling them what to do. This has been accompanied by increased centralization of steward structures, formal recognition of stewards, and the separation of stewards from the members they represent. Emphasis is placed on the skill, experience and expertise of these workplace representatives.

What type of steward?

It is against this background that the role and position of workplace stewards must be understood. Two contrasting models should be considered: first, stewards promoted and controlled by the union; second, the democratically accountable and controlled stewards.

Sponsorship of stewards is a relatively frequent occurrence, particularly in non-manual unions. In this respect, individuals are often sought out by branch officials, senior stewards or equivalent and encouraged to stand as workplace representatives, often subject only to purely formal ratification by members. On these occasions it is expected that stewards will implement union policy and represent union policy, as defined and understood by the sponsor. Where this happens stewards become little more than siphons for policy initiated and generated elsewhere. They act as messengers for members to officials and as conduits from officials to members.

In contrast, democratically controlled stewards are those who have been elected by members, after debate and discussion about the office and/or the candidates. Under these circumstances stewards, in conjunction with members, are more likely to be in a position to initiate and generate policy and activity in the workplace. They will take initiatives and prosecute members' concerns with management and indeed within the union.

No doubt this is a simplistic contrast. Nevertheless, it is possible to see stewards of both types in the way many unions are structured and operate (e.g. the sponsorship of stewards historically in the SCPS compared with the relative autonomy and activity of TGWU stewards in the car industry).

What is often forgotten in arguments about the role and position of workplace stewards is their primary role in unions. It has now been recognized in a number of unions that for effective and representative negotiations on behalf of members there is a critical need for a detailed knowledge and experience of the jobs they do and the problems they face. It has been accepted that there is no substitute for the direct involvement of stewards who come from particular workplaces. Similarly if action is to be considered by members or indeed by national officials involved in negotiations, such plans often come to nothing if stewards are not involved in drawing them up and in helping to initiate local action. In these respects, workplace stewards constitute the most important level of representation in unions. Without them the union is a relatively hollow facade, removed and distant from the membership at work in offices, factories, schools or wherever.

Workplace stewards

The primary rationale for workplace stewards is that effective and democratic organization demands that structures are established whereby members in the workplace can be represented by one of their number, by their delegate. This requires that the following criteria be met:

1 A steward should represent a sufficiently small and coherent group of members to enable routine contact to take place. If at all possible, this should be on a workplace basis, or at worst, a cluster of workplaces in close proximity. It is preferable that a workplace with few members elect a steward to represent their interests than to have none at all (e.g. in the National Union of Journalists [NUJ] a chapel can be established where there are a minimum of four members);

2 Workplace stewards must be elected by the membership and subject to recall by members in the event of not adequately or effectively representing their views. This will ensure a procedure for accountability and control by members;

3 Workplace stewards must sit on branch executive committees so that they can present the views of members to the committee, play a full part in the debate and discussion, and report back to members. Anything short of this means that stewards are bypassed and are not in a position to represent their members' interests;

4 Workplace stewards must have a range of responsibilities. They should have union authority to call members' meetings. They should be the first person whom members contact with questions, problems and demands. They are the members' delegates within the union as well as in negotiations whenever and wherever they occur.

In line with earlier observations about branch organization, the primary rationale of the branch is the organization of collective activity and the provision of opportunities for membership participation and involvement. As such the branch executive committee occupies an important position in the branch. For this reason, it is important that such committees be composed largely of workplace stewards. If this is done, then stewards are able to represent their members' interests directly to the committee, participate in debate and discussions, and report back to members for further decision and action. Through such procedures there is the possibility of developing steward accountability and membership involvement and participation.

Following on from this principle, branch officers should be elected by and from the workplace membership, or by and from the stewards on the committee where the workplace membership cannot meet. While such principles of organization should be maintained as far as possible, it must also be recognized that some branch positions are sufficiently demanding (e.g. secretary) or require specialist interest or application (e.g. treasurer) that such officers should not necessarily act as stewards for a section of the membership. In this way the principles of stewardship should be maintained, namely that the branch committee have detailed knowledge and experience of members' jobs and the problems faced by them. Only under these circumstances, will branch executives be in a position to retain that involvement which means that plans can be drawn up, negotiations conducted and members spoken for within the union, with the confidence of membership support and unity.

In summary then, the key principle of union democracy must be a structure and organization which enable membership participation and involvement. At a minimum, this requires locally-based branches organized around the workplace stewards. While these arrangements will not necessarily guarantee participation and involvement, they do provide the conditions necessary for this possibility.

11. National Union Organization

The same principles of union democracy must inform the organization of unions beyond branches. In this chapter I examine this with reference to the broad contours of union organization at district and regional levels. This is followed by an examination of participation and involvement at a national level focusing on conference, executive committees and paid full-time officials.

Contours of union organization

One of the most striking features of union organization is the degree of variation from one union to another. The chief reason for this is the range of employment structures and associated negotiating procedures that unions confront. All the same many union structures have been sanctified by tradition and the history of different unions (or sections of unions) so that a particular structure may remain unaltered even where management has restructured and reorganized.

The different levels of union organization beyond the branch include district committees, regional or area structures, trade or section organization and national organization. In some unions, regional and district committees have considerable autonomy and authority (e.g. the TGWU and in the past the AUEW(ES)); while in others it is at the national level that most responsibility and authority is exercised (e.g. the SCPS). This raises the question of whether such variation is inevitable or whether certain principles for democratic organization can be enunciated in the light of the above comments about branch and steward organization.

In general, unions must organize so as to be able to negotiate with employers and represent the interests of members. As a result, unions must connect effectively with employment structures in the variety of negotiating arrangements that already exist. This has important implications for the democratic organization of unions.

Two broad distinctions can be made about the kind of negotiating arrangements which exist between employers and unions. On the one hand, negotiations may be highly centralized, conducted at a national level; on the other hand, it is not uncommon for negotiations to be conducted at regional or district, or even branch and workplace level. In either case, of course, unions have to be organized to respond effectively to these arrangements.

In general, the principles underpinning branch organization – participation, involvement and commitment – must be manifest at all levels of unions. Thus it is imperative that links between branches are established so that members can co-ordinate activity, exchange information, provide support to each other and develop the foundation for broadly based collective organization able to undertake collective action in furtherance of members' needs and interests. At the same time, such levels of organization that are developed on this foundation must provide for membership control of delegates and the accountability of these delegates to membership constituencies; otherwise democracy is a charade.

Districts
In view of this, the first level of organization beyond the branch should be the district committee. Such committees should be composed of workplace stewards from a given locality. All workplaces should be represented, irrespective of employer, employment structure, function or grade. These should be the first level of inter-branch membership co-ordination and co-operation.

The purpose of such committees is to provide a forum in which matters concerning all workplaces covered by the district can be discussed, and where necessary acted upon. Questions relating to pay, conditions of work, the community, laws and regulations and state policies should be considered at such committees. In particular, it is through them that the participation and involvement of women members at a local level should be subject to scrutiny. Although this may best be achieved through sub-committees (composed only of women) such bodies should consider these matters in detail and report back to parent district committees for action. Similar principles of organization should apply for ethnic minorities.

The establishment and strength of these committees rest upon the branch organization referred to above. Obviously such committees do exist in many unions, but the decisive feature is their composition. When they are composed of workplace stewards then they are directly responsible and accountable to workplace members. To the extent that stewards are subject to direction and recall by members then the district committees are founded on the best traditions of democratic accountability and control.

Regions

In order to develop a wider consideration of union policy and to provide a democratic basis to national organization, district committees should be grouped into regions. Such a level of organization allows for the broad involvement of members in policy-making and enables the establishment of links between local and national levels of organization. It also allows unions to develop and strengthen relationships with other unions.

Regions should have a general responsibility for organization within the region, for the co-ordination of inter-branch activity (particularly during campaigns), for the consideration of issues across employers (where relevant), for the co-ordination of bargaining and representation, and for the organization of membership meetings and education. Such organization would also facilitate the development of union policy toward regional issues and questions.

At regional level two institutions should be established: a regional conference and a regional committee. First, a regional conference should be held once a year to formulate policy insofar as it concerns the region and to initiate policy for consideration at a national level. Such conferences should be attended by branch delegates from each district committee covered by the region. Second, a regional committee should be established composed of delegates from each district council. These committees should be responsible for administration, negotiation (where relevant) and organizational matters. In this way the principles of democratic accountability and control are maintained. At the same time, provision is made for the articulation and development of policy as seen by members under the auspices of district committees and regions.

It is important to note that in some unions these principles necessarily mean a separation between policy making and negotiation. In some cases negotiation arrangements do not allow for either district or indeed regional involvement, partly because most negotiations are at a local or national level or because they take place under industry or trade auspices. In these circumstances, the district and regional structure is concerned almost entirely with union administration, policy and organization. All the same, this simply reflects a narrowing of the range of concerns at these levels of organization and does not constitute an argument against them.

National conference

The major opportunity for participation at the national level in most unions occurs at conference, usually held annually. There is some variation in the basis for attendance at these conferences, ranging from regional or district representatives to branch delegates. Nevertheless, in most unions conferences are attended by branch delegates.

Ideally the national conference is the opportunity for members via their delegates to express their views about union policy and plans. It is also the occasion when members review past activity. Following on from the principles outlined above such conferences should be composed of branch delegates mandated by members to vote this way or that. Voting at conferences is usually based on two methods: by show of hands or by card vote. The show of hands is simply a count of the number of delegates responding when the vote is called for; whereas the card vote is based on the number of branch members the delegates represent at conference.

It would seem, however, that the card vote is a peculiarly undemocratic form of signifying support for motions. This is not because not all members may have attended the mandating meeting for conference, thereby inflating the significance of those who did. It is because one of the key features of collective organization and action is debate and discussion at meetings, conference and similar occasions. In view of this, the final decision of conference should be based on the show of hands not the card vote. Those delegates who are mandated no doubt vote accordingly; where delegates have been given discretion (e.g. to listen to the debate) then it is right and proper that they should cast their vote as participants in the debate not as participants who are worth more or less because of the size of the constituency they represent.

In this respect, recommendations to submit key motions or issues to a referendum of all members represent another undemocratic practice. Conference is the mass meeting writ small; it is the embodiment of collective practice. In contrast, for all its appearance of involving more individuals in putting a cross on a piece of paper, the referendum signifies merely an aggregation of individual views and opinions and as such does not accord with the collective principles of union democracy.

National Executive Committee

In almost all unions the national executive committee (or equivalent) is the supreme authority of the union between conferences. It brings the union together as it were in order to meet challenges and realize objectives. As such, these committees have considerable power and a wide range of responsibilities in respect of membership, expulsion and recruitment, organization, affiliations, negotiations, industrial action, subscriptions funds and expenses. Additionally such committees usually have an overall responsibility for those paid staff who are employed by the union. In view of the formal authority and responsibility of those committees it is imperative that they are democratically accountable to and controlled by the membership. This takes two forms – by election and at conference.

With regard to election there is an enormous variation in procedures. Such committees may be elected by postal ballots of all members (e.g. the AUEW[ES]), individual branch ballots of members (e.g. the CPSA) area or regional ballots of one sort or another (e.g. the NUR), and branch votes at conferences (e.g. the SCPS). Different procedures may have been the outcome of change and evolution over time or may have been introduced as a result of the political success of a particular grouping within the union, then able to impose its will (e.g. the AUEW(ES)). But whatever their origins, particular practices are nearly always justified by the rhetoric of democracy within unions.

Following on from the principles espoused above, the basis of a democratically elected national executive must be an election procedure which ensures accountability to and control by the membership. This is only possible where the executive members have a constituency to whom they are answerable and from whom they are drawn. It is in this further respect that regional organization is essential. Executive members elected at and by a regional conference are much more likely to be responsive to the needs and demands of members. They can be called to acount, to report and justify their actions and general demeanour as executive members. In these respects, they are rooted in and bound to a constituency of the membership. As for conference, an executive council is usually obliged to report the year's decisions and activity for consideration by delegates. This is clearly an appropriate way to relate to the conference. To this extent, executive committees are collectively responsible for decisions taken.

All the same it is quite impossible for executive committee members to pretend that they are necessarily in agreement on all issues and policies. In accordance with experience, political perspectives, beliefs and traditions, individual executive members may disagree and oppose policy. In a democratic union provision should be made for this disagreement to be recognized and considered. Ultimately all committee members must justify their records to the membership and this cannot be done behind the anonymous cloak of collective responsibility. In the last resort, it is the membership which is collectively responsible for union policies and actions, not a small executive committee which is elected to speak for members' interests.

Thus executive committees should be elected by and accountable to regional constituencies. In this way, such committee members would be inextricably linked to and responsive to the membership. At the same time, so that this link can be made manifest, it is essential that executive committee members are answerable to the membership. This requires that the activities and record of such committees are open and subject to debate and discussion. So on the basis of the individual contribution and activity of committee members, collective responsibility and participation is developed.

Paid full-time officials

It is now possible to consider the vexed question of union bureaucracy, particularly as it applies to national paid full-time officials such as general secretaries (although the remarks below apply in principle to paid district and regional officials). As noted above, such officials have been chosen for particular attention by the major political parties. Specifically, there have been frequent calls for these officials to be elected, usually by a secret postal ballot of all members. The one qualification that has been introduced recently is that where such officials do not have a vote on the national executive committee then appointment rather than election is acceptable.

Within unions themselves there has been a longstanding concern with the methods of appointment or electing paid national officials, particularly general secretaries and related senior officials. As already indicated, a considerable number of general secretaries are already elected, usually for life. Furthermore it is more likely that manual union general secretaries will be elected than those in the non-manual unions. Frequent calls have been made for the extension of election procedures to include currently appointed general secretaries and all paid officials, particularly those who have a direct involvement in negotiations and organizations (e.g. the CPSA).

The argument in favour of election is usually presented in terms of the desirability of making paid officials accountable to the membership. In the absence of such accountability the membership often does not have any control over these officials. As a result, they are liable to dominate and indeed control the affairs of the union. This is particularly so in negotiations and industrial action, where they seem to act as if they should take decisions on behalf of members.

This view of paid national officials may be developed in a more elaborate form with references to their social and political position. Specifically, they acquire an expertise on the affairs of the union which gives them a considerable advantage over the annually (or equivalent) elected executive committee members. Further, the dominant position of these officials is reinforced by the division of labour now typical in many large unions. They also hold office in the long-term rather than in the short-term, as is the case with most executive committee members. Hence, paid national officials often provide a considerable degree of continuity and stability in the union thereby reinforcing their own positions.

Against this it has been argued that such officials develop interests and concerns which are removed from the experience of members and, in the words of Michels, are 'diametrically opposed' to members' interests. In other words it is often argued that even the most progressive officials, once appointed or elected for life, become seduced by the trappings and privileges of leading a union and they forget past commitments and beliefs. This arises because of the nature of their jobs, the people they associate with, their income, standard of living and the political approach they develop and come to espouse; they become union bureaucrats.

In recognition of these tendencies, many have argued that paid national officials should be subject to regular and periodic election. Others have argued the contrary view, namely that appointed officials who are elected for life are to be preferred because in many unions the security of national office means that they can advocate progressive and radical policies, often against the background of a less politically developed and progressive membership.

But what is the political significance of such elections? In general, it must be said, that while elections for paid national officials are a condition for democratic unionism they are imperfectly so. This is because such elections cannot be based on the principles of membership participation and involvement. The reason for this is that the constituency for such elections must be the whole union membership. This requires that some type of individual or block ballot be conducted. As a result, the principles of accountability and membership control depend upon the single thread of the election. There is no necessity – and no real room – for membership participation and involvement.

More than this, such elections tend to reinforce the current dominant position of paid national officials. Where unions elect their general secretaries, the candidates necessarily subject themselves to a national plebiscite of the union membership. Under such circumstances the election itself becomes the primary form of accountability. But there is no other direct means of membership control, with the result that such officials are in a position to claim the mandate of the periodic election or, indeed, the one election that placed them in that position for life to justify their actions and commitments.

The alternative of election at conference is also unsatisfactory. Although conference is the embodiment of the membership, and this could be seen to be an appropriate forum for the periodic election of such officials, currently it serves to reinforce the supremacy of the individual rather than the collective leadership of the union. Such elections would come to highlight the virtues and strengths of the individual candidate and not the virtues and strengths of the national executive committee as the collective embodiment of the union between conferences. For this reason, this alternative must be rejected.

The more important issue is to *control* these officials via national executive committees. As noted above it is possible for these committees to be directly accountable to and controlled by membership constituencies. It is these committees who should act to control and instruct paid national officials. But with the encouragement of employers as well as the media, and partly because of prevailing union structures, this happens too seldom. More often it is the paid officials, whether elected or appointed, who control executive committees, take the lead in negotiations, and are seen to guide and control union affairs. It is this relation which needs to be reassessed.

In suggesting this, the problem then becomes one of the relationship between paid national officials and national executive committees as well as the procedure for the election of individual officials. It is not really possible to reinforce and develop democratic control and accountability by an election procedure; rather, it is necessary to focus on the quality and character of the relation between paid full-time officials and executive committees. In this respect the leadership of the union must be the responsibility of the committee and not the individual general secretary. Paid officials should be, in the words of formal union rhetoric, servants of the union. In practice this must mean that national paid officials are subordinate to the national executive committee.

The problem of course, is that today many national executive committees would find such a reversal of relationship unnerving, to say the least. For too long, executive committees (with some honourable exceptions, like the Associated Society of Locomotive Engineers and Firemen: ASLEF) have been used to being told what to do and, indeed, to say. This must be changed. For this to happen national executive committees must themselves be subject to democratic control in the way outlined above, paid full-time officials should be appointed and should be actually rather than formally subordinate to such committees. In this way the basis for democratic control and leadership will be provided.

Such a development would mean that the jobs done by general secretaries (and associated officials) would change. At a general level the executive committee would become the collective embodiment of the union. In line with the principles outlined above the spokesperson for the union would be the president, elected from and by the national executive committee. Thus the general secretary (and associated staff) would be subordinate to this body. Rather than spokesperson for the union, the general secretary would become a genuine functionary answerable and responsible to the national executive committee.

By focusing on relations rather than on the procedure for election and appointment the foundation for union democracy can be laid. Although this will not solve the problems associated with paid full-time officials it does mean that these problems could begin to be sensibly addressed. More than this it is to claim that the only way to confront the tendency for such officials to acquire over-powerful positions is to deal with the basis of this power rather than the thin strand of appointment or election.

For union democracy to flourish the principles of participation and involvement must be made part of union organization beyond the branch. This means challenging and questioning many of the procedures and practices evident in unions. For left-wing activists it means making difficult choices about what to campaign and fight for in the quest for democratic practice and procedure. Nonetheless fighting for these principles lays the foundations for union democracy.

12. Union Democracy and Socialism

The argument presented throughout this book is that union democracy is about membership participation and involvement, even at the highest level of the union. This is a view that runs counter to most of the current arguments on the subject. In the main, as I have made clear, advocates of union democracy have presented a view which draws on key features of parliament as its hallmark. This however, represents a denial of union democracy, relying as it does on notions of membership aggregation and representation rather than participation and involvement.

More specifically, there is an argument that the Trade Union Bill 1983 and other similar legislative proposals pose a major threat to unions which must be resisted. Without doubt, the ability of unions to defend and advance workers' interests will be weakened by the substitution of membership involvement and participation by secret individual ballots and related procedures. Not only will unions be weakened in their defence of 'economic' issues, but also they will be demobilized as potential vehicles in the struggle to create a socialist society.

Unions and the state

It is important to recognize at the outset that unions have been shaped and moulded by the procedures and processes of collective bargaining. They are structured and organized so as to secure pay settlements and negotiate about the conditions of work. This has meant that while they have been relatively successful in working within the structures of capitalism, their potential to oppose these structures and organization remains unfulfilled.

To a certain extent a distinction can be drawn between the public and private sector. In the case of the latter there has been a long tradition of local bargaining alongside national bargaining procedures. For many, local workplace activity came to signify the potential of unions as members and their local leaders successfully negotiated and campaigned for a degree of autonomy over pay levels (piece-work bargaining) and conditions of employment. But these developments were not as widespread as is often thought, being confined principally to the car and engineering industry. Moreover, even these died away as the economic depression undermined the basis for confident local action. Alongside this, in many unions there has been a trend toward the centralization of pay bargaining. This has been accompanied by re-organization, with the result that today there is widespread recognition of stewards as well as integration into formal union structures of the previously fairly autonomous steward committees and similar bodies.

In the public sector it is possible to discern a movement in the opposite direction, namely from highly centralized structures to the sponsored introduction of an element of local workplace organization and autonomy. Historically there has been a long tradition of centralized bargaining structures in the public sector, often resulting in a close relationship between the structure of management and that of unions. Negotiations have usually been conducted under the auspices of statutory arrangements, such as standing bodies which review pay and conditions, the Whitley systems of joint negotiating committees or a miscellany of other similar arrangements covering other areas of public sector employment, including the nationalized industries. Although there has been a tradition of local activity, reflected also in union organization, in the mining industry, large sections of public employment have been devoid of a local union activity, and indeed organization until fairly recently.

Over the last decade and a half many of the state sector unions have challenged the basis of established negotiating procedures. To a large extent, this has been prompted by government initiatives with regard to the state sector. Briefly, these developments include a massive restructuring of the state sector, through cuts and cash limits, reorganization and abolition of established collective bargaining structures, the selling off of sectors of the state apparatus and managerial and grade reorganization. The result has been job insecurity, undermining conditions of employment, low wage settlements and the demobilization of formerly confident union members.

It is in the context of these developments that state sector unions began to take a leading part in the labour struggle, particularly throughout the 1970s. Many were involved in strike action, often for the first time in their history. As the form and character of the welfare state was challenged, many of these unions began to campaign on its behalf. Cuts campaigns involved publicity, demonstrations, lobbying and local industrial action. Partly in order to meet these challenges, a number of unions examined their structures and organizations with a view to strengthening themselves at local level through the introduction of steward systems and so on.

This meant that many unions have broadened their concerns and preoccupations beyond the narrow economistic objectives of the past. The issue for both in the private and public sector is now quite clear and two alternatives are emerging:

Either to meet the current challenges by opting for a strong centralized union in which membership participation is generally kept to the occasional casting of a secret individual vote, preferably a postal vote, with a leadership exercising care and caution in the defence of wage levels and conditions of employment. (In some circumstances it may even be appropriate to heed those voices which accept the need for some reduction in living standards. Where necessary, the political fight can be carried forward under the auspices of the Labour Party. This may even require intervention against too great a radicalism emerging in the party.)

Or to meet the current challenges by insisting that, at a minimum, unions are organized and structured in a democratic way. More than this, it is precisely when organization is threatened and members' standards of living undermined that unions must reorganize according to democratic principles. Difficult decisions must be taken, old views recast, old loyalties reassessed. So, union objectives must be broadened. This will require participatory decision-making, and an involved and committed membership. Union solidarity must be constructed, the members' awareness and understanding of the class issues developed. It is only under the circumstances of union democracy that this will be at all possible.

Unions and socialism

The argument in favour of union democracy can now be extended to encompass socialism. In this respect union democracy represents both the embodiment of socialist practice and the prospect that socialism can be achieved. To an important extent then, union democracy and socialism are inextricably linked together.

As argued throughout the book, a properly democratic union is one which is defined in terms of collective organization and action. This is the hallmark of union democracy and it is a minimum condition for socialism if socialist practice is to mean anything. In this sense union democracy defines socialism and vice versa.

Thus to the extent that union democracy is manifest, union practice anticipates in an embryonic form the mode of organization and operation characteristic of a socialist society. In such a society decisions will be taken on the basis of collective discussion and agreement, debate and consideration. Moreover, at all levels, in all areas of social organization the representatives of the working class will be accountable to and controlled by that class. It is this that distinguishes socialist organization and practice from that in all other societies.

Within capitalist society, unions represent one of the few examples of this form of organization and mode of practice. They are inherently collective organizations. It is on this basis that they pose a challenge to capital. The power of capital depends upon encouraging competition between workers: the unemployed and the employed; gender conflict; racism, and competition for individual status and rewards. To the extent that employers are successful in this they are strengthened and the working class further divided and subordinated. Against this, collective organization is the only way that the unity of workers can be institutionalized so that workers have some means of countering the power of capital.

The reason that there is such a wide-ranging debate and discussion about union democracy among union members is that the link between unionism and socialism has not always been recognized or acknowledged. Nevertheless, one of the key ways that this recognition may be developed is through the experience of participating in a democratic union. Through participation and involvement in meetings, or by acting as delegates for the union membership, it is possible to experience first-hand the trappings and privileges of socialist organization and practice. Through debate, discussion and careful consideration of issues and policies, individual members play their part and put their point of view. And, at the end of their deliberations, decisions are made, delegates selected, and the membership bound by the collective decision. This is union democracy and socialism in practice.

Of course, not all decisions will be the most desirable, not all delegates be the most appropriate. Mistakes will be made, decisions regretted. After all the attempt to achieve union democracy, to learn from experience and to extend the margins of the union, occurs in the context of capitalist society. It occurs in situations where people do feel insecure, where other needs and requirements seem equally important, where peculiar procedures have been established and sanctified by time and practice. Nevertheless despite these difficulties union democracy does represent hope for the future.

Union democracy

It is only through union democracy that the concerns of unions will genuinely be broadened. In many unions it has become relatively easy for progressive policy to be formulated and agreed. This has meant winning over conferences and executives to a particular point of view. However, such policies are a charade when they cannot be translated into campaigns supported by a majority of members. Too often the fortuitous meeting with a receptive politician or employer, the publication of policy, the issuing of press statements become substitutes for campaigns. Only when policies are the product of a participating and involved membership will they be fought for by the majority rather than the active minority.

The future of healthy, independent and autonomous trade unions depends on the ability of unions to build and maintain collective forms of organization and participation. This means that union delegates must be controlled by and accountable to the union membership. It also means that policy determination must be subject to collective consideration and decision. The means for achieving this is through the workplace meeting, the joint committees of workplace delegates, and delegation to all levels of the union.

Thus unions must give attention to trade union democracy, to the forms and procedures of collective participation and organization, and ultimately to the circumstances and conditions for union solidarity and unity. By taking these crucial steps toward realizing the collective ideal, unions will not only ensure that they are in a position to defend and extend the interests of their members but also lay the foundation for realizing the long-term interests of the working class. And if socialism is not about that, it is not about anything. So, union democracy is both the condition for and the means to socialist organization and practice.

A Guide to Reading

Chapter 1

There are surprisingly few recent publications about union democracy. One exception is the very readable marxist contribution by Richard Hyman in *Marxism and the Sociology of Trade Unions*, Pluto Press, 1971. In his booklet, Hyman considers the classic marxist debates about unions including contributions by Marx and Engels, Lenin, Trotsky and Gramsci. He also reviews the classic orthodox contribution to the debates by Michels in 1911 as well as more recent academic studies on unions. Apart from this, much of the literature on union democracy has been fairly arid, concerned with the processes of decision-making and the like. The primary aim has been to develop models of democracy and to discover signs of democracy in unions.

To learn where the Tories have come from the two best publications to read are: Inns of Court Conservative Unionist Society, *A Giant's Strength: Some thoughts on the constitutional and legal position of Trade Unions in England*, 1958; Conservative Political Centre, *Fair Deal at Work: The Conservative approach to modern industrial relations*, 1968. These two publications should be complemented by the recent Green Paper, *Democracy in Trade Unions*, HMSO 1983, Cmnd 8778. Perhaps the best commentaries on the Tory threat to trade unions are the many Labour Research Department publications, including: LRD, *Our Unions, Our Democracy*, January 1983; LRD, *Union Freedoms Under Threat*, July 1983; LRD, *Unions Attacked*, December 1983. Significantly, the LRD has developed a more and more critical analysis of current union practice. Equally important, and in the best traditions of investigative journalism, Patrick Wintour over the last few years has provided a series of penetrating articles on trade union organization and action, first in the *New Statesman* and, more recently, in the *Guardian*.

Chapter 2

The major political parties have shown little reluctance to set down their views and when given the chance to translate them into legislation. They are as follows:

Conservative Party

The most important policy statement published by the Conservative Party which set the terrain of the debate within the party is Inns of Court Conservative Unionist Society, *A Giant's Strength: Some thoughts on the constitutional and legal position of Trade Unions in England*, 1958. The publication, ten years later, of Conservative Political Centre, *Fair Deal At Work: The Conservative approach to modern industrial relations*, 1968, represented a development and up-dating of some of the basic ideas set down in the earlier document. More recently, the Conservative Party in government has produced two Green Papers and a White Paper, each of which addressed the question of legislation aimed at controlling and restricting trade unions. They are entitled: *Trade Union Immunities*, HMSO 1981, Cmnd. 8128, *Democracy in Trade Unions*, HMSO 1983, Cmnd. 8778; and *Proposals for Legislation on Democracy in Trade Unions*, Department of Employment, July 1983.

A very general warning of Tory Party concerns when in office was given in Conservative Central Office, *The Right Approach: A statement of Conservative aims*, 1976.

Alongside these statements, Tory governments have legislated on trade unions as follows: Industrial Relations Act 1971; Employment Act 1980; and Employment Act 1982. At the time of writing the Trade Union Bill 1983 is going through parliament and is likely to be on the statute books before October 1984.

Labour Party

The most important statement by the Labour Party is in the form of a White Paper, *In Place Of Strife: A Policy for Industrial Relations*, HMSO 1969, Cmnd. 3888. Whereas the proposals embodied in the White Paper were seen by many trade unionists as an attempt to restrict and limit militant trade union action, subsequent legislation was welcomed as protecting unions and guaranteeing rights in employment. This apart, the Labour Party frequently commits itself to working with trade unions through legislation and policies in support of 'working people'. Statements to this effect abound in election manifestos.

Six acts should be noted: Health and Safety at Work Act 1974; Trade Union and Labour Relations Act 1974; Sex Discrimination Act 1975;

Employment Protection Act 1975; Trade Union and Labour Relations (Amendment) Act 1976; and Race Relations Act 1976. In part, the Labour government proposed this legislation in return for voluntary wage restraint by trade unions.

Labour Party intellectuals have occasionally gone into print to lay out the case for union 'reform' or to defend unions against accusations from the Tory Party and others. Perhaps the most well-known publication defending the view that union action is not the reason for rising inflation rates is D.Jackson, H.Turner and F.Wilkinson, *Do Trade Unions Cause Inflation?* second edn., Cambridge University Press, 1976. For a clear statement in favour of union 'reform' by a current Labour Party Member of Parliament, see G.Radice, *The Industrial Democrats: Trade unions in an uncertain world*, Allen & Unwin, 1978.

Alliance Parties

The first comprehensive statement advocating compulsory postal ballots was published by the SDP in 1982, SDP Trade Union Reform Policy Group, *Reforming the Trade Unions: a new deal for Britain*, 1982. This was followed by a 'White Paper', published in December 1982, by SDP Council for Social Democracy, *Industrial Relations: 1 trade union reform*, 1982. What is noteworthy in these documents is the strong advocacy of corporatist industrial relations policies for Britain, in many ways a hangover of past Labour Party commitments.

The Liberal Party has published relatively little on trade union organization. It has been more concerned with the general position of trade unions, outlining a case for 'industrial partnership', for example, N.Hawkins and I.Fordyce, *Liberal Action on Industrial Relations: A Positive Role for Trade Unions*, n.d.

Other reading

No examination of Party policies and legislation would be complete without a consideration of the Donovan Report: Royal Commission on Trade Unions and Employers' Associations, 1965–68, *Report*, HMSO 1968. This report became a major point of reference for subsequent policies and legislation. The accompanying research papers provide argument and data on trade union organisation and practice.

One important source for learning the views and opinions of politicians is the weekly *Hansard*, HMSO. It is, for example, very illuminating to read the extensive debate at the time of the Second Reading of Trade Union Bill: see House of Commons Parliamentary Debates, *Weekly Hansard*, HMSO, 3 November 1983. These publications contain verbatim reports of all parliamentary debates and are very revealing of the nuances of official party policy as well as the opinions and prejudices of individual Members of Parliament and the Lords and Ladies of the Realm.

Commentaries on legislation are numerous. The most useful and comprehensive book on employment law for workers is J.McMullen, *Rights at Work: A Workers' Guide to Employment Law*, second edn, Pluto Press, 1983. Other commentaries about specific pieces of legislation which are useful, include: B.Weekes, M.Mellish, L.Dickens and J.Lloyd, *Industrial Relations and the Limits of Law: The Industrial Effects of the Industrial Relations Act, 1971*, Basil Blackwell, 1975; and R.Lewis and B.Simpson, *Striking A Balance? Employment Law after the 1980 Act*, Martin Robertson, 1981.

Chapter 3

Although the TUC has been relatively mute on the question of union structure and organisation, in 1983 it was moved to the view that the Tory threat was real and published TUC, *Hands Up For Union Democracy*, May 1983. The TUC position that there are many paths to democracy is elaborated in this publication. Complaints are also made about the unfairness of the proposed Trade Union Act.

Quite recently, there are signs that the Tory strategy of creating an uncertain climate whereby unions will look to their organization and reconsider their traditional alliances has had an effect on TUC views. This is evident in the publication TUC, *TUC Strategy*, January 1984, prepared under the guidance of Lionel Murray for the TUC General Council. The focus of the document is on the need for unions to reassess their appeal to workers, consider reorganizing more directly around the workplace and to reaffirm the traditional TUC view that the TUC must deal with all governments.

Chapter 4

Arguments about union bureaucracy often derive their inspiration from the now classic statement by R.Michels, *Political Parties: A Sociological Study of the Oligarchical Tendencies of Modern Democracy*, Free Press, 1962. Although it is a study of the German Social Democratic Party, then the largest such party in the world, before the First World War, the argument has been drawn on to analyse trade unions. One of the best known, interesting and accessible studies in this tradition is S.Lipset, M.Trow and J.Coleman, *Union Democracy: The Internal Politics of the International Typographical Union*, Free Press, 1956. This is a detailed and careful study of printworkers and their union in New York. With reference to Britain, see J.Edelstein and M.Warner, *Comparative Union Democracy: Organisation and Opposition in British and American Unions*, Allen & Unwin, 1975. Whilst Lipset, Trow and Coleman were pessimistic about the possibility of union democracy Edelstein and Warner are more optimistic about this possibility. Edelstein and Warner focus principally on the constitutional arrangements in unions which may enhance or inhibit union democracy. Unfortunately, it is not an easy book to read, although much of the detail is in itself interesting and important. One other study which is worth looking at is J.Hemingway, *Conflict and Democracy: Studies in Trade Union Government*, Oxford, 1978. It is especially interesting for the discussions about the seamen and bus-workers.

An historical account of British trade unionism which raises a number of questions relevant to a consideration of union bureaucracy and democracy is T.Lane, *The Union Makes Us Strong: The British Working Class, Its Trade Unionism and Politics*, Arrow Books, 1974. Lane defends trade unionism as a progressive force, although he also argues that trade unions cannot be a substitute for a socialist political party. He is especially interesting in his discussion of the tensions which shop stewards may experience as well as the dilemmas often faced by union leaders.

Chapter 5

There is a paucity of up-to-date empirical detail about trade union structure and organization. To an important extent this has been eased with the publication of J.Eaton and C.Gill, *The Trade Union Directory*, second edn., Pluto Press, 1983. This book provides details about union history, union officials, organization, workplace activity, external relations, policies, and recent events involving all TUC unions. It is an indispensable reference book. Additionally, the LRD in its many publications makes available information about current union practice and concerns. Alongside this, it is worth looking at some of the studies of specific unions for further detail about election practice and procedure. The study by Edelstein and Warner referred to above has details about elections for the NUM and the AUEW (ES).

Chapter 6

Until recently, the information on workplace trade unionism has been limited, focusing on particular industries. The best such study is without doubt Huw Beynon, *Working For Ford*, Penguin, 1984. Beynon's is a rich and penetrating study of the Ford Halewood plant, which provides valuable insights on workplace trade unionism.

With the publication of W.Daniel and N.Millward, *Workplace Industrial Relations in Britain: The DE/PSI/SSRC Survey*, Heinemann, 1983, a valuable source on workplace trade unionism is available. This report (and any subsequent reports) is likely to become a basic reference tool.

Chapter 7

There are a number of publications which address the apparent separation by unions between 'economics' and 'politics'. Among the more interesting and important contributions to the discussion are: A.Flanders, 'Trade Unions and Politics' and 'What Are Unions For', in A.Flanders (ed.), *Management and Unions*, Faber & Faber, 1970; and L.Minkin, 'The Party Connection', *Government and Opposition*, autumn 1978. A readily accessible and interesting survey of this question is K.Coates and T.Topham, *Trade Unions In Britain*, revised edn., Spokesman 1980.

Chapter 8

There is considerable debate about the problems with unions as well as the problems they face. The most comprehensive range of left-wing views about unions today can be found in M.Jacques and F.Mulhern (eds), *The Forward March of Labour Halted?*, Verso in association with *Marxism Today*, 1981. Many of the contributions to this book were first published in *Marxism Today* in response to the controversial article by Eric Hobsbawm under the title 'The Forward March of Labour Halted?' *Marxism Today*, September 1978. A range of political views are canvassed in the book, including left Labour Party, Communist Party, and Socialist Workers Party.

Recently, attention has been drawn to the fact that industrial action by some workers can adversely affect the working class. In particular, strikes and the like by state workers can be especially harmful to those who depend on the state. These issues are examined in a very cogent way in London Edinburgh Weekend Return Group, *In and Against the State*, Pluto Press, 1980.

Another related study which looks at the experience of health workers is J.Neale, *Memoirs of a Callous Picket: Working for the NHS*, Pluto Press, 1983. Neale examines the very real difficulties of organizing and campaigning in situations where workers are separated and divided from each other as well as where the people most immediately affected by industrial action are not employers but patients.

One historical study which is especially illuminating on the question of sectionalism is H. Turner, *Trade Union Growth Structure and Policy: A Comparative Study of Cotton Unions*, Allen & Unwin, 1962. In this book Turner examines the relationship between employment structure, organizing strategies and trade union organization. Although a lengthy book, it is well worth reading.

A large number of books have now been published on women and unions. Among the very best introductions to this field is C.Aldred, *Women At Work*, Pan, 1981. This, plus the book by Jenny Beale, *Getting It Together: Women As Trade Unionists*, Pluto Press, 1982, present strong and convincing cases that women are a force for democratic trade unionism who will enrich trade unions through their participation and involvement.

Richard Hyman has long written on issues about union democracy. His article 'The Politics of Workplace Trade Unionism: Recent Tendencies And Some Problems For Theory', *Capital and Class*, no. 8, summer 1979, represented a development of his ideas with reference to workplace trade unionism. Unfortunately, there has been little attempt to engage directly with the questions he raises.

There is a considerable literature which advocates the view that unions are basically reformist organizations which, together with the Labour Party, are important vehicles for the gradual improvement and betterment of capitalist Britain. The major exponent of this view is Hugh Clegg, particularly in *The System of Industrial Relations in Great Britain*, third edn., Basil Blackwell, 1976.

It is important to remember that many of the debates about the problems with unions are long standing. Many of the problems referred to in this book are mentioned in G.D.H.Cole, *Organised Labour: An Introduction to Trade Unionism*, Allen & Unwin and The Labour Publishing Co. Ltd., 1924. Too often the problems of trade unionism are assumed to be new or of temporary duration. Cole provides a salutary reminder that this is often not the case.

Chapter 9

Useful reading which takes up issues considered in this chapter includes H.Braverman, *Labor and Monopoly Capital: The Degradation of Work in the Twentieth Century*, Monthly Review Press, 1974; R.Hyman, 'Trade Unions: Control and Resistance', *People and Work*, Open University, 1976; and E.O.Wright, *Class, Crisis and the State*, New Left Books, 1978.

A recent reader which contains a selection of contributions on the debates about white-collar workers and unions is R.Hyman and R.Price, *The New Working Class? White-Collar Workers And Their Organizations*, Macmillan, 1983.

An important publication in which the relation between class and gender hierarchies is examined is C.Cockburn, *Brothers: Male Dominance and Technological Change*, Pluto Press, 1983. In this study of the print industry Cockburn shows the way in which men use their control of work to the disadvantage of women. She presents a case that the restructuring of the print industry could be the occasion to transcend sectional and sexual self-interest. But, this would require a major rethinking of the way unions organize and operate. Similarly, Sallie Westwood details difficulties women face when confronted by patriarchial union structures within a textile factory in her book, *All Day, Every Day*, Pluto Press, 1984.

Trade unions have a disgraceful record on the involvement and participation of black members in union organization and activity. Two books which deal with different aspects of this question are P.Braham, E.Rhodes and M.Pearn (eds), *Discrimination and Disadvantage in Employment: The Experience of Black Workers*, Harper & Row, 1981, and A.Sivanandan, *A Different Hunger: Writings on Black Resistance*, Pluto Press, 1981. Sivanandan, in particular, has long raised questions about the discrimination and exploitation of black people at work and elsewhere.

Chapters 10 and 11

Much has been written about the role and significance of shop stewards. This literature has addressed the origins of stewards, the scope and significance of steward activity, and the importance of stewards for union organisation and action. Recently there has been a wide-ranging debate about the current role of stewards. This debate was sparked off by Tony Lane, in an article entitled 'The Unions: caught on the ebb tide', *Marxism Today*, September 1982. He argued that unions face immense problems arising from a changing industrial environment as well as problems associated with internal union organisation. In this article Lane questioned the tendency for stewards to become removed from the day-to-day concerns and experience of members. Unfortunately, the rejoinders to Lane tended to dwell on his characterization of stewards, rather than taking up some of the substantive issues raised by the article.

Whilst the Lane debate raised important questions, the best recent examination of shop stewards is by Michael Terry in G.Bain (ed.), 'Shop Steward Development and Managerial Strategies', in *Industrial Relations in Britain*, Basil Blackwell, 1983. Michael Terry examines the basis of shop steward organization and action with reference to the deepening crisis of British capitalism. In this respect, he makes a particularly significant contribution to an understanding of the recent history of shop steward development and organization.

Chapter 12

A number of the ideas developed in this book were first formulated in the course of a commissioned review of trade unions. The two relevant publications are P.Drake, P.Fairbrother, R.Fryer and J.Murphy, *Which Way Forward? An Interim Report for the Society of Civil and Public Servants*, Department of Sociology, University of Warwick, 1980; and P.Drake, P.Fairbrother, R.Fryer and G.Stratford, *A Programme For Union Democracy: The Review of the Organisation and Structure of the Society of Civil and Public Servants*, Department of Sociology, University of Warwick, 1982. These arguments were further developed in a booklet on union ballots, P.Fairbrother, *The Politics of Union Ballots*, WEA, 1983.